History
Fieldwork

F. J. Johnson & K. J. Ikin

Macmillan

Acknowledgements

The authors and publishers wish to thank the following who have kindly given permission for the use of their pictures:

Aerofilms: p.15 (bottom), p.18, p.22, p.24, p.30, p.32, p.36, p.46, p.60
Hallam Ashley: p.5 (bottom)
Barnaby's Picture Library: Victorian middle-class home, p.63, p.64
The British Tourist Authority: p.7, p.15 (top), p.41
The Department of the Environment: p.9, p.33
The Mansell Collection: p.43
Norwich Corporation and P. Armes: a medieval street, p.63

The Peak Park Planning Board: p.5 (top)
The Radio Times Hulton Picture Library: p.44, Georgian houses, p.63
J. K. St. Joseph, Cambridge University Collection: p.8, p.13, p.20
J. Sainsbury & Co. Ltd: back cover
Walter Scott: p. 42
K. Simmonds: p.39, p.56 (top)
George Wimpey and Co. Ltd: a modern housing estate, p.63, nineteenth-century working-class homes, p.63, redevelopment of slums, p.63
Reece Winstone, Bristol: p.56 (bottom)

Any remaining photographs are from the authors' own collections.

© F. J. Johnson and K. J. Ikin 1974

First published 1974

Published by
MACMILLAN EDUCATION LTD
London and Basingstoke

Associated companies and representatives throughout the world

Printed photolitho in Great Britain by
Ebenezer Baylis and Son Limited
The Trinity Press, Worcester, and London

Contents

Preface

This book arose quite naturally out of studies done with a school Local History Society. The work was then extended and adapted as part of the general history course of a Leicestershire High School.

The authors believe that fieldwork is an integral part of history teaching. It adds an extra dimension to history, it is in itself a stimulus to interest, it relates the subject to reality and as part of environmental education it helps to create an understanding of what lies around us.

The books are intended as supplementary work to improve awareness and understanding, and may be used as part of a thematic or a chronological approach to history. They can certainly be used for individual or group project work, not only in history but in integrated humanities courses and environmental studies.

Many of the questions in the fieldwork and classwork exercises are open-ended. Such questions do not have right and wrong answers but require the pupil to think for himself, to give opinions and suggestions and to answer at length. It is intended that the student should use his imagination in an historical setting not only in answering questions but in asking further questions for himself.

It cannot be emphasised too much that the value to be derived from fieldwork visits is in proportion to the amount of preparation done beforehand by both teacher and student. The more background knowledge a pupil has on the subject in general and the more information on the precise historical circumstances of a particular site he or she possesses, the more meaningful will be the fieldwork.

1 Early Man

The last two thousand years of British history are often called the period of recorded history because the people of these times have left written records about their lives. Prehistory is the name given to the half-a-million years before then, during which no written records were made. In those remote centuries, our distant ancestors were very slowly making discoveries and learning to live together in settled groups. They were becoming civilised. By careful study of what can still be found of these people we can picture how their life must have been.

The Life of Early Man

1 By far the longest period of prehistory is called the Stone Age. Man was then a nomad. What does this mean? Why did he have to lead this sort of life?

2 Early men were very different from us. What did they look like? Find out how they changed through the ages. What advantages did they have over the apes?

3 During this time there were several periods of intense cold. What were they called? Until about ten thousand years ago our country was joined on to the rest of Europe. Now of course, we are an island.

4 These early people often chose to live in caves in hilly districts. Can you think of four reasons why they chose caves for their homes? What other sorts of homes did they have? They would have had to build these.

Life in Caves

Look carefully at the picture of a cave scene.

1 Why was fire so important to prehistoric people? How was fire first discovered? How did they keep it alight from day to day?

2 What animals did they hunt for their food and how were they captured? When we say that many of these creatures are now extinct, what do we mean?

3 Besides meat, what else could prehistoric people eat?

4 How did they clothe themselves?

5 What pictures are sometimes to be seen on the walls of their cave homes? Draw some of your own.

6 Man the hunter became man the farmer when he learned to tame animals and grow his own crops. Once he made these discoveries, why did his life become easier and more comfortable?

7 What was a quern used for? How were the earliest pots made? Eventually woven cloth replaced earlier garments. How was the weaving done?

A cave site: Thor's Cave,
Dovedale Manifold Valley, Derbyshire

Fieldwork at a cave site

1   Describe the area outside the cave as it appears today.

2   Do you think the place would have looked the same many thousands of years ago?

3   Water was as necessary to the people living in the Stone Age as it is to us. Where would they have got their water from? How would they have carried it?

4   What sorts of things would you expect might be discovered in the cave? What *has* been found? Where are the objects now?

5   Draw a plan or sketch of the site.

6   Describe the inside of the cave. Try to imagine how unpleasant it must have been for our remote ancestors who lived here—the isolation, the cold, the damp, the uncertainty of day-to-day life, the fear. Write down your feelings while you are actually on the site.

Grimes Graves

1   Flint is a common stone found in most parts of England. Examine closely a piece of flint and decide why men in the Stone Age chose flint for tools and weapons.

2   What is the difference between a flake and a core tool? Draw pictures of flint tools such as scrapers, borers, sickles and cleavers.

3   Describe how the axes and spears were fastened to the wooden hafts.

4   In addition to flint, what materials did prehistoric people use?

5   By the New Stone Age better tools were needed and thus only the best quality flint would be used. One area where this is found is the Thetford and Brandon region of Norfolk. Find this on a map. Here are some of the finest prehistoric remains in England— factories for producing flint. Why, for

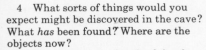

Inside Grimes Graves, Norfolk

A reconstruction of Grimes Graves

hundreds of years, did local people call these pits Grimes Graves?

6   Look carefully at the pictures. Why was the mine so much wider at the top than at the bottom? Why do you think the miners dug through several seams of flint before beginning to mine?

7   How was the mining done? What did they use for picks and shovels? How did the miners get into the pit and how was the flint brought out? Why were the flint galleries not very long? What happened when a mine was worked out?

8   What does bartering mean? Many examples of tools made from Norfolk flint have been found in other parts of the country. What does this suggest?

5

Early Man—His Death

A barrow is an ancient grave. There are two main types, the long barrow and the round barrow. The former were built during the New Stone Age and the latter in the Bronze Age.

The earliest long barrows were simply earth mounds built over a wooden shelter

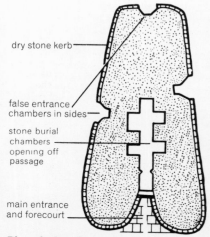

A long barrow

- alse entrance
- earth covering
- main entrance
- dry walling
- paved forecourt

where the bodies were collected and stored before being buried together. The barrow was then sealed. In later centuries stone barrows were built and then gradually filled—rather like a family vault of more recent times. Later still, during the Bronze Age, round barrows began to replace the earlier long barrows. The dead were usually buried in these after being cremated.

These graves tell us much about the lives of early men.

Long Barrows

1 The builders obviously put a great deal of effort and time into preparing these tombs to care for their dead. What does this tell us about their beliefs?

2 Explain how the barrow in the sketches was built.

3 What ceremonies do you imagine would take place in the paved forecourt?

4 Objects buried with the dead are often found in these barrows. What sort of things would they be? Why do you think they were there?

5 Why were false entrances often built into the barrow?

6 How has the appearance of many of these barrows changed over the last few thousand years?

7 What names are given to the clumps of stones which are left? Legends have grown up about such stones. If you can find one, write it down.

Plan of a long barrow

- dry stone kerb
- false entrance chambers in sides
- stone burial chambers opening off passage
- main entrance and forecourt

Plan of a long barrow

Round Barrows

1 What is meant by cremation? How was this done?

2 What were cinerary urns used for?

3 Find out and draw the different types of round barrows. Why were they so shallow compared with long barrows?

A dolmen or cromlech

Fieldwork at a barrow

1 Which type of barrow is this? How was this particular barrow built? What was it used for? When would it have been built?

2 What other types of barrow were there? How did they differ in structure from this one?

3 Where were the materials brought from to construct this tomb?

4 Make a sketch of the barrow as it looks today. Make notes of how the surrounding area has changed since the barrow was built.

5 Find out whether any excavation has taken place and what has happened to any 'grave goods' which were found.

6 Is this an isolated site or is it part of a group of prehistoric remains? If the latter is true describe them.

7 Take any necessary measurements to make a model or plan of the site.

2 Henges

About four thousand years ago, towards the end of the New Stone Age, man began to build circles of large upright stones. Inside the circles, which were often large and complicated, our distant ancestors worshipped. We call these circles 'henges' and can think of them as the first temples or churches in our country.

Stonehenge

This is the most famous of all the prehistoric remains in Britain. To help you answer these questions you will need a map of southern Britain and any book which tells the story of Stonehenge.

1　The building of Stonehenge began about four thousand years ago and took over five hundred years to complete. Our great cathedrals were also built over many centuries. How did this affect the buildings? The same happened to Stonehenge.

2　We know very little of the builders. There were several different groups of them. The first are often called the 'Beaker Folk' after their pottery. If these people did not get a good harvest they would starve. What would they pray for? Why was the sun so important?

3　The earliest circle was of blue stones, each of which weighed about four tons and came from the Prescelly Mountains in South Wales. How can we be sure that this is where the stones

came from? How far are the mountains from Stonehenge? How would these heavy stones be carried today and along which route would they come? How do you think they would have been carried in those days? Would the route have been different?

4　There was considerable trade between the Beaker Folk and the bronze-smiths of Ireland. Does this give us any idea why they chose stones from the Prescelly Mountains for their holy circle? Look carefully at your map.

Above: Stonehenge as it would have looked when built

Left: Stonehenge as it is today

5　The other huge stones in Stonehenge came from much nearer: the Marlborough Downs, only about twenty miles away. To move each stone, weighing about fifty tons, over one thousand men must have been employed. How would this labour force move the stones? How were these great stones made to stand upright? Find out how the lintels—the stones lying on the top—were joined together. There are many similarities between Stonehenge and the temples of Ancient Greece and probably, even in those early days, people from Britain and the Greeks were trading together.

6　Think of the date when this temple was built. How do we know that the worshippers were not Christians? What stories are told of the altar stone in the centre? Legends wrongly link the Druids with Stonehenge. Find out what you can about them.

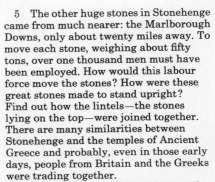

Arbor Low, Derbyshire

On a visit to any henge monument you could do many of the things suggested in the exercise on Arbor Low. In addition here are several other pieces of work:

1   Working in pairs, take measurements of all the main features of the henge in order to draw your plan to scale.

2   Find out where the stones came from and say how they might have been brought to the site.

3   Prepare an account of any excavation, finds and the history of this particular monument. Describe its condition today.

4   Sketch the area as you think it would have appeared three to four thousand years ago.

Arbor Low, Derbyshire: A Bronze Age Temple

1   What does the word 'low' mean? How long ago was Arbor Low built?

2   Prepare a plan from the photograph and label the outer bank, the ditch, the inner stone circle, the barrow and the two entrances.

3   This is a remote, moorland part of Derbyshire. How has this helped to preserve the monument?

4   Few people live near here today. What does the size of the temple suggest about life in this particular area at that time?

5   What have been the effects of the weather on the ditch and the bank?

6   Approximately how many stones are there in the inner circle? What sort of stone would you expect them to be? Remember this monument is in north Derbyshire.

7   What do you think the outer bank was for?

8   What do you notice about the position of the stone slabs? What does this suggest? What were the centre slabs for?

9   What has happened to the barrow near the entrance at the top of the photograph?

3 Hill Forts

The last of the prehistoric periods is known as the Iron Age and it was during this time that the first fortified camps were built in Britain. These are the Iron Age hill forts, the remains of which are still to be seen crowning hilltops in many parts of the country.

1 How many thousands of years ago was the period called the Iron Age? How did it get its name? How long did it last?

2 The people who lived then are often called the 'Ancient Britons'. They were made up of many different tribes, like the Red Indians in America. What are the names of some of the Iron Age tribes? Which one lived in your part of the country? Why did they need to build these great fortified hill camps?

3 There are several different types of camps or forts; promontory forts, cliff castles, contour camps, plateau forts. Find out the differences between them and make sketches of each one.

4 Where did the tribes live when they were not using the forts? Why? Can you suggest why the forts needed to cover so large an area of ground?

5 How would they set about building the fort? What would cause difficulties?

What would their building tools be made of? What was the earth used for, which was taken from the ditch? How were the palisades made?

6 What were the buildings like which were constructed inside the fort? Their water supplies probably came from 'dew ponds'. What were these and how were they made?

7 In times of trouble what weapons were used?

An aerial view of Maiden Castle, Dorset

Maiden Castle, Dorset

This immense hilltop fort covering forty-five acres of ground was first built about 250 BC. More fortifications were added in the following two centuries, making it one of the largest and most elaborate forts in the whole of the country.

1 In which part of Britain is Dorset?

2 Which type of hill fort is this one?

3 When it was first built it was fairly small. Identify the extent of the first fort. Why was one of the sides then easy to attack? How did the later builders try to stop this happening?

4 How many main lines of ditches and banks can you see? Which weapon was invented about two thousand years ago that made these several lines of defence necessary?

5 How were the two gates reinforced? Where was the main entrance? Why were two entrances necessary?

6 Draw a map of the fort and mark

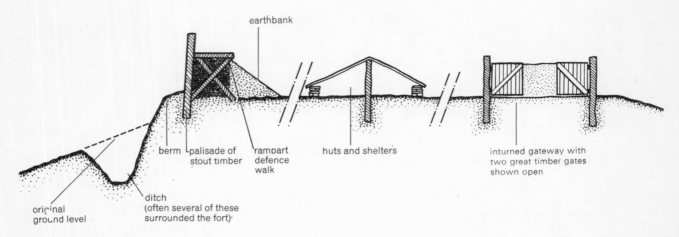

earthbank

berm — palisade of stout timber — rampart defence walk — huts and shelters — inturned gateway with two great timber gates shown open

original ground level — ditch (often several of these surrounded the fort)

Section through an Iron Age hill fort (not to scale)

on it the ditches, banks and gates and the first fort.

7   Maiden Castle fell to the Romans during the first century AD. About three hundred years later they built a small pagan temple in the fort. Imagine you are a Roman soldier coming through the ruined British fort to worship here. In his words, describe what he is thinking of the scene around him.

Fieldwork at a hill fort

1   Describe carefully the position of the hill fort and explain why you think it came to be built on this particular site.

2   Make a sketch map of the earthworks. Show clearly which are ramparts and which are ditches and mark the entrances.

3   Take measurements to enable you to draw a section through one part of the defences. Why are your measurements of depths and heights likely to differ from the original ones? If an accurate site plan is available, it would be useful to compare your findings with this.

4   Pace out the area enclosed by the fort and mark this on your map too. Huts were probably built in this area so that the people from the valley settlements could take shelter in times of attack. What would these huts have been like? What is likely to be left of them? What could be done to prove that they were once there?

5   Find out if the main entrance to the fort is inturned. What does this mean? Why was it built in this way? Were any other special precautions taken to guard the entrance?

6   Are there any signs of postern gates into the fort? What were these used for?

7   Is any side of the fort more open to attack than the rest? Why? Are there any extra defences here?

8   Are there any signs of later development, such as stone walling?

9   Are there any local stories about the fort? Do the local people have any special names for the site?

10   Imagine yourself approaching this fort two thousand years ago. Prepare notes and sketches of the scene as it would have appeared then, including such things as the buildings, the earthworks, the people and the surrounding area.

4 Roman Roads

During the three-and-a-half centuries of the Roman occupation of Britain, many roads were built. These roads are our best reminder of Roman times, for many can still be seen today. Some have modern roads built over them, while others can be traced along footpaths, parish boundaries and the edges of fields.

1   What were the main reasons why the Romans built these roads?

2   Who were the people who built the roads? For example, who were the engineers, who supervised the construction, and who provided the labour?

3   Find out precisely how a Roman road was made. Describe the road-building in detail from the marking-out of the line to the laying of the final surface.

4   How did the engineers keep the road running straight?

5   Why did a road often change direction at high places along its route?

6   Draw a map of the known Roman roads in your area.

7   Why did the Saxons allow these roads to fall into disuse?

8   When was the next good road system built in Britain? What were these roads called?

A Roman road then and now

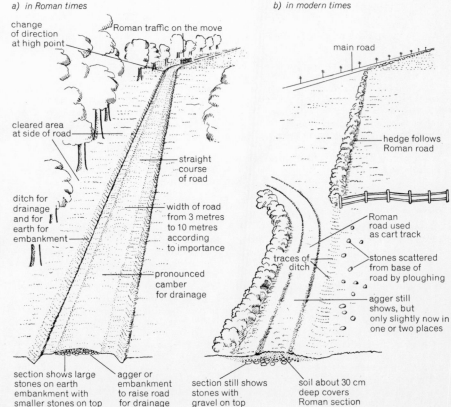

a) *in Roman times*

change of direction at high point

Roman traffic on the move

cleared area at side of road

straight course of road

ditch for drainage and for earth for embankment

width of road from 3 metres to 10 metres according to importance

pronounced camber for drainage

section shows large stones on earth embankment with smaller stones on top

agger or embankment to raise road for drainage

b) *in modern times*

main road

hedge follows Roman road

Roman road used as cart track

traces of ditch

stones scattered from base of road by ploughing

agger still shows, but only slightly now in one or two places

section still shows stones with gravel on top

soil about 30 cm deep covers Roman section

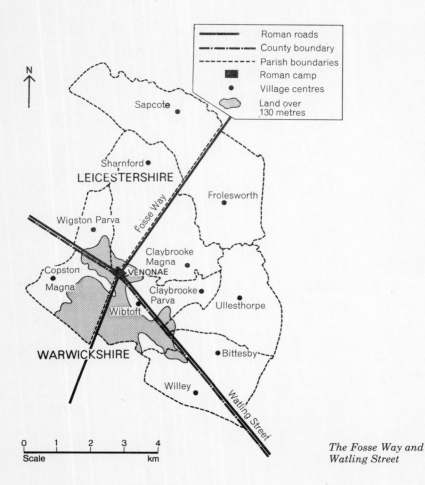

The Fosse Way and
Watling Street

12

The Fosse Way and Watling Street

These two important Roman roads crossed in the Midlands at Venonae, a Roman camp. After the Romans left Britain, the invading Saxons did not use large stretches of the roads. However, the roads could still be seen and made useful boundaries.

1   What covered most of the countryside in the Midlands when the Romans built their roads? What difficulties would they have faced in building them?

2   Find these two roads on a map of Roman Britain. What important places did they link up?

3   Suggest a reason why the roads changed direction at their junction.

4   How does the position of the villages show that the Saxons did not use the Roman roads?

5   How can you tell from the map that parishes and counties came later than Roman roads?

6   What boundary did Watling Street become at the Peace of Wedmore in AD 878?

7   Look up the meanings of the endings of the village names. Which groups of people named these villages?

8   From a large-scale road map or Ordnance Survey map find out what types of road follow these Roman roads today and whether or not a village continues to exist on the site of Venonae.

Ermine Street at Dubrovivae

1   Find Dubrovivae on a map of Roman Britain. What is the nearest large town today?

2   Using the sketch as a guide, find the following Roman features in the photograph:
a. Ermine Street   b. King Street
c. the town walls of Dubrovivae
d. the bypass round the town
e. streets within the town

3   Crop marks are the only means of seeing some of these features. What are crop marks? Why do they show up at certain seasons of the year?

4   What is the striking feature of the course of the Roman roads? What places could be reached by the two roads shown? In how many ways are the Roman roads used today?

5   How much time passed between the building of the Roman roads and the building of the Great North Road? What was the state of road building in Britain during this time?

6   When was the Great North Road built? What type of road was it? Who was the engineer in charge? How is its course different from Roman roads?

7   What can we learn of Roman planning from the photograph?

Ermine Street at Dubrovivae

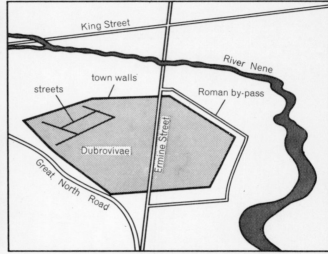

Diagram to show Ermine Street at Dubrovivae

Fieldwork at a Roman road

Before you set out, find out how the road fitted into the Roman road system of Britain. What towns did it link up?

1 Study stretches of the road where there are good remains of the aggar (that is, where the road is not used as a modern road and the remains are raised above the level of the surrounding land). Measure the width of the road at various points. What is the average measurement? Does the width vary much from this? Note any traces of the ditches.

2 Draw a map to show the different places where the road changed direction. Why were these particular places chosen?

3 Sometimes Roman roads had to go round obstacles or zig-zag up steep hillsides and across streams. Find examples but do not mix them up with the major changes of direction referred to in question 2.

4 Pause on a quiet stretch of the road and think of it in Roman times. How far are you from the nearest Roman town or fort in each direction? Imagine armies and civilian traffic on the move. What would this traffic be like? How far would it travel in a day?

5 Show the present-day uses of the road on a detailed map.

6 On suitable stretches look for evidence of stone scatter.

7 A Roman road is an archaeological feature a school group could usefully excavate to find details of its construction. However you must seek guidance in this, and not attempt to dig without an expert in charge.

8 Although much of the Roman road system is known, there is still much to be discovered. You could try to find the line of a 'lost' stretch by examining probable routes on the map and on the ground. Such a find would be a worthwhile contribution to historical knowledge.

5 Roman Fortifications

Britain was occupied by the Romans for nearly four hundred years. The remains of this military conquest and long occupation are to be seen in the many camps and forts throughout the country and in the great boundary walls to the north, Hadrian's Wall and the Antonine Wall.

Hadrian's Wall

Hadrian's Wall is the most spectacular Roman fortification in Britain. It stretched for eighty Roman miles right across the country from coast to coast and marked the northern border of the Empire. Built by the Emperor Hadrian to stop raids by tribes from the north, it was a complete success. In over three hundred years it was overrun only twice and both times the Roman troops had been taken away from the wall.

If you are fortunate enough to visit it, you can examine details of how the wall, with its milecastles, turrets, ditch and vallum, was built. By taking accurate measurements you will see how much of the wall has disappeared over the centuries and how much of the ditch and vallum has been filled in. A walk along the wall will help you to appreciate its commanding position and to imagine Roman soldiers pouring out of the many gates to attack an advancing enemy.

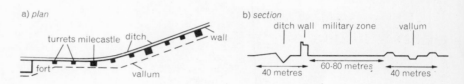

a) *plan*

turrets milecastle ditch wall
fort vallum

b) *section*

ditch wall military zone vallum
40 metres | 60-80 metres | 40 metres

Wall patrolled from milecastles and turrets. Tactics were to attack the enemy from gates in milecastles and forts and to trap them against the wall.

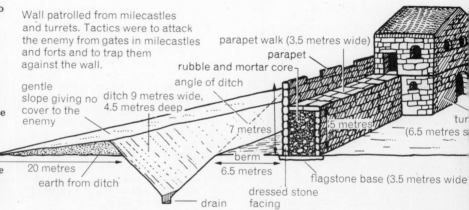

gentle slope giving no cover to the enemy

ditch 9 metres wide, 4.5 metres deep

angle of ditch

20 metres
earth from ditch

7 metres

drain

berm
6.5 metres

dressed stone facing

parapet walk (3.5 metres wide)
parapet
rubble and mortar core

5 metres

flagstone base (3.5 metres wide)

tur (6.5 metres s

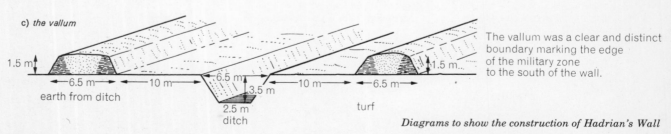

c) *the vallum*

1.5 m
6.5 m | 10 m | 6.5 m | 10 m | 6.5 m | 1.5 m
earth from ditch | 3.5 m
2.5 m ditch | turf

The vallum was a clear and distinct boundary marking the edge of the military zone to the south of the wall.

Diagrams to show the construction of Hadrian's Wall

14

Hadrian's Wall

A Fort of the Saxon Shore: Richborough Castle, Kent

Richborough (Rutupiae) is a most important Roman site. The various lines of fortification and the other remains represent different centuries of Roman building.

1 Here the four Roman legions landed for the conquest of Britain in AD 43. Who was the emperor who ordered the invasion? Who was the commander of the forces? Look for the following two features in the photograph connected with the conquest:
a. Part of the original line of defensive ditches built by the invaders.
b. The huge cross-shaped base of the giant marble memorial built forty years later to commemorate the conquest.

2 In the second century, houses were built here. The foundations of two stone houses can be clearly seen. Do you think this would have been an important military site?

3 The earth fort of the third century is the innermost line of ramparts. How many ditches and embankments are there? What shape are the corners? Were Roman forts usually that shape? Why?

4 The outside ramparts and the stone wall are the remains of a fort of the Saxon Shore. Why and when did the Romans build these forts? Discover the names of other examples.

5 Each fort of the Saxon Shore was near a river mouth or important harbour. Look up the position of Richborough. Why was this place chosen? What has happened to the coast here since Roman times?

6 The only means of communication

Richborough Castle, Kent

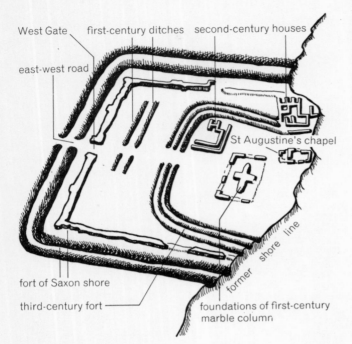

West Gate   first-century ditches   second-century houses

east-west road

St Augustine's chapel

fort of Saxon shore

third-century fort

foundations of first-century marble column

former shore line

A plan of Richborough Castle

6   Draw detailed sketches of the defences of the fort similar to those shown earlier in the book for Hadrian's Wall.

7   Look for traces of Roman roads associated with the fort.

8   Imagine you are a Roman soldier from a far distant part of the empire such as Carthage in North Africa. Write a letter to a friend or relative describing your life here. Give your opinions about the fort, the surrounding countryside, the weather and the people of the native tribes.

for most Saxon Shore forts was by sea, for the main Roman roads were usually some way away. However, Richborough is an exception and the road leading from the West Gate is a very important one leading to Canterbury and London. Which road is this and where does it lead to beyond London?

7   The later Saxon chapel was to commemorate the landing of St Augustine. When did he land? Why is he important in English history?

Fieldwork at a Roman fort

1   Find out when this Roman fort was built and why it was needed. Show your findings on a map.

2   As with all military works such as Iron Age hill forts and later castles,

the first thing to do is to study the site. Why was this particular place chosen? Look first at its general position. Does it command wide views and dominate the countryside?

3   Look at the lie of the land where the fort was built and see if any use was made of small natural features such as rising ground and streams. Did they help to make the fort stronger?

4   Has it the usual shape of a Roman fort? Look for evidence of gates and any remains of buildings inside the fort. Make a plan using exact measurements of the remains.

5   By reading about Roman forts, work out where different buildings might have been and add them to your plan to show how the fort would have appeared when it was in use.

6 Motte and Bailey Castles

These were the first true castles to be constructed in England. The earliest ones were built immediately after the Norman Conquest as strongholds in which the Norman lords could live in safety and from which they could control the locality.

1 What was the main difference between a castle and a hill-camp or a fortified town?

2 William, Duke of Normandy, became king of England in 1066. Why would he order the building of large numbers of these castles in his new country?

3 Why was it possible to build them quickly?

4 An essential part of the castle was the motte. Suggest the two ways of obtaining a motte.

5 In what part would the owner of the castle live? Why? Explain carefully what extra defence this part had. Do you think his living quarters would have been very warm and comfortable?

6 We know that many of these castles were prefabricated. What does this mean?

7 Why were these castles usually made of timber and not of stone? What might have happened to the motte if heavy stone had been used? Which people would have been commanded by the Normans to build them? What would have been the weakness of wooden castles in time of attack?

8 What different buildings were found in the bailey or courtyard? How was this area defended?

9 By the twelfth century there were hundreds of these castles in England. In which parts of the country would they be most common? Why?

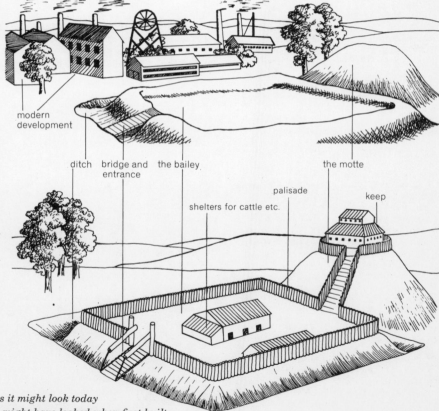

Above: the site of a motte and bailey castle as it might look today
Right: the same motte and bailey castle as it might have looked when first built

10 Why, in most cases, are the earth mounds all that is left of motte and bailey castles? What do names like Castle Street and Castle Field tell us?

11 Find out how motte and bailey sites are marked on Ordnance Survey maps and draw up a list of those in your area.

Fieldwork at a motte and bailey castle

1 Before making the visit prepare a sketch map of the site. A large-scale Ordnance Survey map should help.

2 Walk across the length and breadth of the site and mark on to the map the main features such as the motte, the bailey and the main entrance. How does the Ordnance Survey map show ramparts and ditches? Mark on your map where these can be clearly seen and where they have disappeared. Also record where you think other features, such as the keep and the inner fence, would probably have been.

3 Draw a section right across the site to show as many features as possible. Pace out and calculate the area.

4 Measure the ditches and banks as accurately as you can. Suggest why your findings are likely to differ considerably from the original measurements.

5 Were there any special reasons why a castle had to be built here? For example, does it defend a river crossing, a valley or a town?

6 Did the builders make use of any natural features, such as rivers, marshes or steep slopes, as part of the defence? Describe them. Was any side more open to attack than the others? Were any extra defences built on this weak side?

7 From where would the water supply for the castle have come?

8 Are there any known records of stone buildings here? While on the site make a careful search and record the position of any stone remains. Was the stone quarried locally? What usually happened to any stonework on sites like this?

9 Why did some castles become more important than others? Why do you think this castle did not develop into one of the great strongholds of the later Middle Ages?

10 Imagine this site in the early Middle Ages and describe an everyday scene, with its noise, smells and colour. Include the comings and goings of the different folk: soldiers, villagers, the miller, the blacksmith, the lord—perhaps setting out to go hunting.

11 You should be able to find out by research whether any excavation has taken place here. If so, what were the results? Write your own account of the known history of the site.

Pleshey Castle

This is a good example of how a small motte and bailey castle looks today many hundreds of years after it was first built. Using the drawings at the start of the chapter as your guide, draw the castle as you think it would have looked and label the following parts:
a. the motte
b. the bailey
c. the keep
d. the position of the palisade
e. the outer ditch
f. huts for cattle and horses
g. the entrance to the bailey

Pleshey Castle, Essex

7 The Deserted Village

Deserted villages occur in most parts of England but mainly in the Midlands and the east. They are villages which were occupied in the Middle Ages but were then abandoned for various reasons. In some cases there are bumps and hollows in the ground to show where the village once stood. In others there is little or nothing left to see.

Why villages became deserted

1   From the Black Death in 1349, successive outbreaks of bubonic plague cut the population of the country by one third and completely wiped out some villages.

2   Sometimes when this happened in good farmland, other peasants on poor land left their own villages to go and live there. The poorer villages then decayed.

3   The demand for English wool grew in the fifteenth century, especially from the continent. Landowners, including the great monasteries which owned land, realised they could make vast profits from sheep and turned whole villages into sheep pastures, forcing out the people and pulling down their houses.

4   This eviction was easier where there were few freeholders, that is, where there were not many peasants who owned their own land.

5   Some villages were pulled down so the landlord could make or enlarge a deer park.

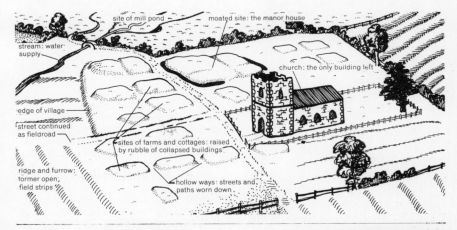

Above: a deserted village as it might look today

Right: the same village as it might have looked in the Middle Ages

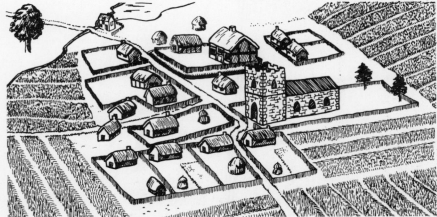

19

surrounding open fields. Draw pictures of everyday life in the village.

10 Does anything at the site suggest why it was abandoned? For instance, is it in the park of a country house or did it become the grange farm of a monastery?

11 Fields have names. Are the names of the modern fields connected in any way with the deserted village? The one in the photograph is called 'town field'.

12 Is the site supposed to be haunted? Find out the story.

An aerial view of Hamilton, Leicestershire

Hamilton: A deserted village in Leicestershire

Nine or ten families lived in Hamilton before the Black Death. These were reduced to four by 1377 and the small village had completely disappeared by 1450.

The aerial photograph shows all that remains of the village today.

Fieldwork at a deserted village

The best sites to explore are those with earthworks which can easily be seen on the ground. Even these sites are more readily understood if an aerial photograph or a large-scale Ordnance Survey map of the remains is available.

1 Find the edge of the actual village where the open fields started. Record any earthworks which separate the village centre from the ridge and furrow of the open fields.

2 Explore the hollow ways and work out the former street pattern. Which is the main street? Did any streets continue through the open fields? If they were more than field roads, to which villages would they lead?

3 Measure selected house plots and compare their size with your house and garden. What buildings other than houses would have been on the larger plots? Look for gateways trodden down to street level.

4 Can the site of the manor house be seen? If it is moated, measure the width and depth of the moat. Look for traces of stonework. If there are any, write down what sort of building stone it is.

5 Record any details of the church if it still exists.

6 Map the ridge and furrow around the village. Blocks of strips all running in the same direction were called furlongs. Mark any of these on your map.

7 How far is the village site from a stream? Look for evidence of a mill or fishponds.

8 Draw a map of the village in as much detail as possible.

9 Imagine the scene some six hundred years ago, both in the village and the

8 Monasteries

Ruins of monasteries great and small are to be found in all parts of the country. At the height of the Middle Ages there were over nine hundred monastic houses. Starting as small centres where groups of men could live together in a devout and religious way, they often became wealthy institutions through grants of land, property and money.

1 Why did some men become monks in early Christian times?

2 Why is Saint Benedict so important in the story of the monasteries?

3 Make a list of monastic orders, saying when and why they were founded.

4 What were the vows taken by monks? What did they mean?

5 What was the difference between an abbey and a priory?

6 How did the life of a friar differ from that of a monk?

7 Make a list of the many ways monasteries served the rest of the community. Who is responsible for this now?

8 How did monasteries become such wealthy places?

9 Why were people becoming critical of the monasteries towards the end of the Middle Ages?

10 What was the dissolution of the monasteries?

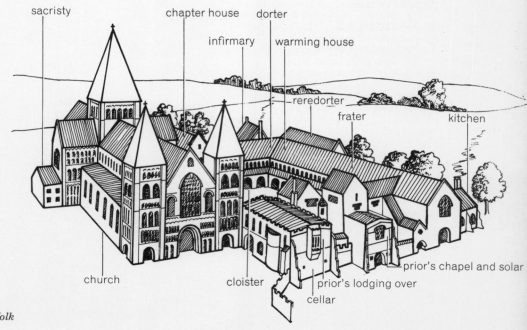

A reconstruction of Castle Acre Priory, Norfolk

Fountains Abbey

The remains of this great abbey are to be found in Skeldale, Yorkshire. It was founded in 1132 by monks from St Mary's, York.

1   The trees in the photograph mark the slopes of the valley which contain the monastery. Why would an isolated valley in the Yorkshire hills be chosen by the monks?

2   From the photograph identify each part of the building which is labelled in the plan.

3   Describe in detail the purpose of each part of the abbey.

4   From the position of the church, work out the direction the camera was pointing.

5   On which side of the church were the cloisters and the other buildings? Why was this side usually chosen?

6   Fountains Abbey was a Cistercian monastery. What does this mean? Cistercian monasteries had choir monks and lay brothers. What was the difference between the two groups? Does this help to explain why the church is such a long building?

7   What was the work of the chamberlain, cellarer, almoner, infirmarian, hospitaller, and sacristan? In which part of this monastery did each of them work?

8   Why did the warming room have the large chimney? Which other parts of the abbey would have chimneys?

9   The river was diverted so that it passed under parts of the abbey. For what purposes would the abbey have used the river?

10   Why is a famous monastery like this in ruins?

An aerial view of Fountains Abbey, Skeldale, Yorkshire

22

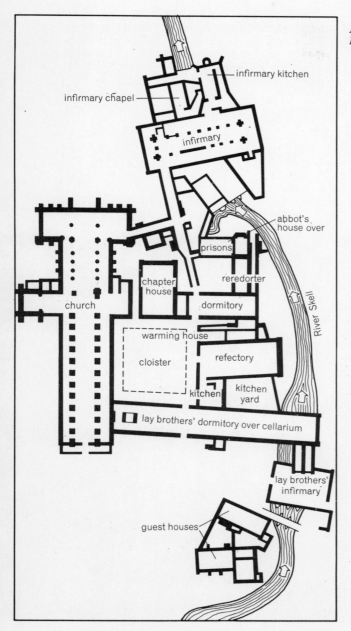

A plan of Fountains Abbey

Labels on plan:
- infirmary kitchen
- infirmary chapel
- infirmary
- abbot's house over
- prisons
- reredorter
- chapter house
- dormitory
- church
- warming house
- cloister
- refectory
- kitchen
- kitchen yard
- lay brothers' dormitory over cellarium
- lay brothers' infirmary
- guest houses
- River Skell

Fieldwork at a monastery

1   Tour the remains of the monastery and work out what each part was used for. Label each part on a plan of the monastery.

2   Choose one of the parts of the monastery and imagine a scene there five hundred years ago when the buildings were in use. Make notes for a full description of the scene, the activity and the everyday routine there.

3   Working in groups, record details of striking and interesting features of any part of the building which is still standing.

4   In the grounds of monastic sites the places where the monastery gardens and fish ponds once were can often be seen. Find and record what can be traced of these and say what their importance would be.

5   Study the setting of the monastery and carefully describe its position. Try to picture what it was like when the monastery was founded. Suggest reasons why that particular place was chosen. For example, was it close to a town or was it deliberately built in an out-of-the-way place?

6   Look at any buildings on the site which were built after the dissolution of the monasteries. What materials from the monastery were used in these buildings? What sort of buildings have succeeded the monastery? What is their condition now?

7   Make a record of any other items which have a special connection with the history of the place, both when it was a monastery and afterwards. Look for such things as monuments, graves, and coats-of-arms.

8   Nearly every monastery has a written guide and history. Use this to find out as much as you can about what is known of the monastery.

9 The Parish Church

Religion has always been a very important aspect of people's lives. The centre of the religious life of the parish was naturally the church, and as most English churches are very old they are in themselves a record of history, of changes and events throughout many centuries.

The Church Exterior

1   What is a lych gate? What does the name mean? Can you see one in this photograph?

2   As usual in churchyards, there are several evergreen trees and shrubs. From pagan times these have been taken as a sign of everlasting life. What other reason is often given for having yew trees in churchyards?

3   There are few graves to be seen on the north side of the church. There was an ancient superstition about this. Find out what it was.

4   What is meant by consecrated ground? Which people were not allowed to be buried in consecrated ground?

5   Churchyard memorials such as gravestones only came into general use towards the end of the seventeenth century. Where were memorials to the dead of wealthy families placed before then?

6   Many churchyards are now being cleared of their memorial headstones which are often being arranged around the edge of the grounds. Why do you think this is?

7   The photograph shows a fine broach spire. Note its eight sides which make it more elegant and less exposed to the wind. In what ways would a parapet spire be different?

8   What are buttresses for? Note the angle buttresses on the tower. In what ways would diagonal, clasping and flying buttresses be different?

9   Identify the following parts of the church: the nave, the chancel, the porch, the south aisle and the north aisle.

A parish church

The Interior of the Parish Church

Here are some details of the inside of a parish church to help you with your investigations.

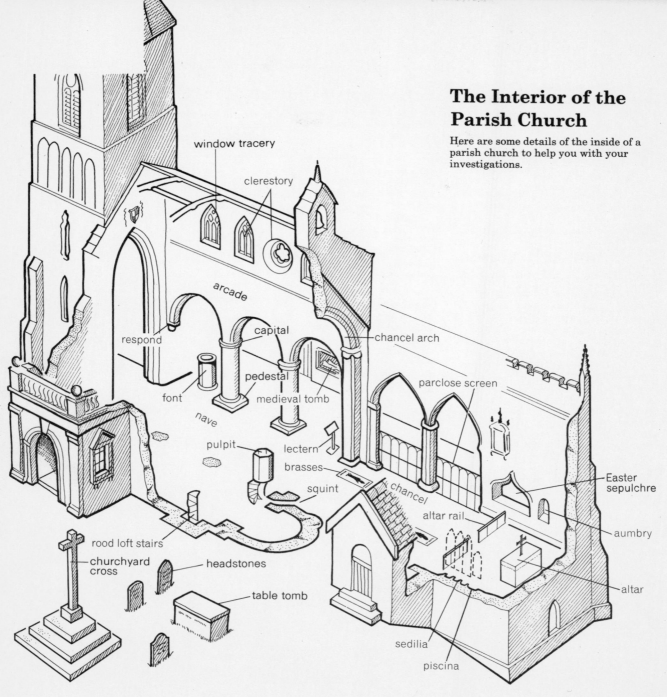

window tracery

clerestory

arcade

respond

capital

pedestal

font

medieval tomb

nave

pulpit

lectern

brasses

squint

rood loft stairs

churchyard cross

headstones

table tomb

chancel arch

parclose screen

chancel

altar rail

Easter sepulchre

aumbry

altar

sedilia

piscina

Plan and Development of the Parish Church

The changes in the plans of church buildings which have taken place over the centuries record the changes in the story of the church. Some of this story is outlined here but you must use one of the many reference books on churches for greater detail.

Aisles were added as the population grew and villages became more wealthy. When times were prosperous the villagers often spent a lot of money in rebuilding and enlarging their church.

Key to building periods

Plans of churches are usually shaded to show the time when the particular parts were built. The dating refers to the first few feet of stonework above the ground: a higher part could be later in date.

 Norman – 12th century

 Early English – 13th century

Perpendicular – 15th century

Victorian – 19th century

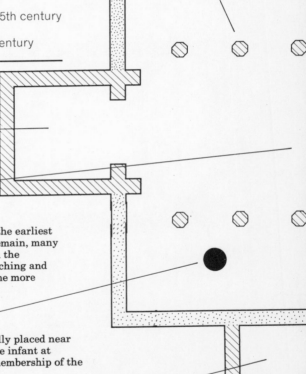

The nave is the body of the church. In medieval times the congregation stood during services, and only the old and sick were seated on stone benches around the walls. Space was needed for the processions which formed part of many services. The nave had many other uses. For example, plays were performed there. The earliest religious dramas, often part of the service, developed later into miracle and mystery plays. Village meetings were certainly held there, and markets and fairs, usually held in the churchyard, occasionally strayed into the nave. Even church ales—village celebrations at which locally brewed beer was drunk—were held in the nave. The nave of the church was in fact the village hall of today.

Seating in the nave dates from the Reformation when the services were longer. The first benches were sometimes replaced by box pews to keep out draughts, for there was no heating in churches. The modern seating is often from the nineteenth century when it was put in by Victorian church restorers. In fact in their enthusiasm these Victorians were often as drastic in their alterations as reformers and Puritans had been before. They often replaced pulpits and lecterns and removed rood screens to clear the view to the altar.

The tower A splendid tower, perhaps capped with a *spire*, also featured in prosperous rebuilding. Soaring to heaven to the glory of God, a tower was a source of envy to neighbouring villages.

The pulpit and lectern Of the earliest pulpits and lecterns which remain, many date from the Reformation in the sixteenth century when preaching and reading from the Bible became more important.

The font is traditionally placed near the door to represent the infant at baptism entering into membership of the church.

The porch, designed as a protection against the weather, became increasingly used for village business, such as signing documents and agreements. Some porches have an upper storey for this.

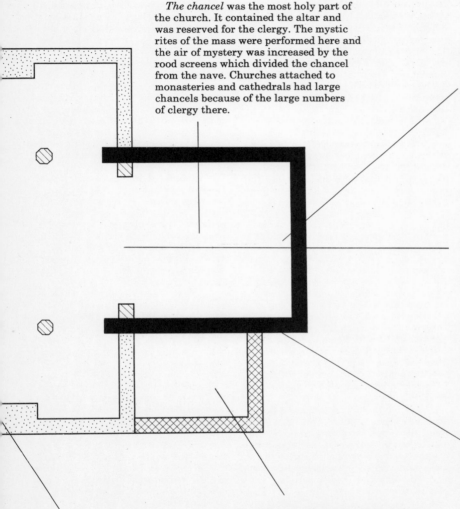

The chancel was the most holy part of the church. It contained the altar and was reserved for the clergy. The mystic rites of the mass were performed here and the air of mystery was increased by the rood screens which divided the chancel from the nave. Churches attached to monasteries and cathedrals had large chancels because of the large numbers of clergy there.

The altar is usually at the east end of the chancel. Medieval stone altars were often broken up at the Reformation and replaced by wooden tables nearer the nave. They were moved back again in the seventeenth century and were railed off in Victorian times. Other altars could have existed in aisles and side chapels.

The chancel arch separates the chancel from the nave. Across this opening was the *rood screen* which took its name from the cross or *rood* above it. This life-size crucifix had a wooden gallery or *loft* in front where candles were burned and musicians played on some occasions. The *rood loft stairs* gave access to this loft. *The doom painting* often filled the space above the chancel arch and showed what would happen on the Day of Judgement. This shows how very different the interior of a medieval church was from a modern one: then *pictures* adorned the walls and colour was everywhere. People could not read and as the services were in Latin they learned many of the Bible stories from pictures. Roods, wall paintings and much stained glass were removed at the time of the Reformation and later by the Puritans in their desire to remove idols and popish symbols.

Piscina—a basin in the church wall in which communion vessels were washed after use. A piscina in an aisle means there was an altar nearby.

Sedilia—stone seats for the clergy helping with the mass.

Medieval tomb Only wealthy and important families were commemorated inside the church. Some tombs are dated and their decoration provides information on dress and armour.

The vestry is for the priest to dress or 'vest' himself and keep the communion plate and registers. The chancel was used for these purposes in the Middle Ages so these rooms are usually a modern addition to the church.

Fieldwork at a parish church

1 Write down your first impression of the appearance of the church. For example, is it small or large, tall and graceful, or squat and compact? What impression of colour does the building material give it? Describe the church among its surroundings.

2 The position of the church gives clues to the history of the area, but these clues are difficult to work out and you will have to ask your teacher about it. For example, with a village church, look to see if it is in the centre or at one end of the village. Does the church stand on its own? If it is a town church, is it one of many and where is it in the town?

3 Examine the outside of the church. Draw and label details of the way the walls are built. Does the style change with the different stages in the building? What is the chief building material? Where does it come from? Is it commonly used in the area?

4 Record details of the tower— buttresses, parapet, bell-openings. Is there a spire? What type is it?

5 Most churches were built in stages with additions and alterations taking place in different centuries. The different styles of architecture are proof of this. Draw, or photograph where possible, samples of the church architecture. Look especially at a. the windows and their tracery; b. the doorways; c. the arches between nave and aisle and between nave and chancel; d. the columns with their pedestals and capitals; e. the clerestory. The identification of the style of these features from reference books will help you with the key to the building periods on your plan.

6 Make an outline plan of the church, measured as accurately as possible. Record the position of the various features of the church as you study them. Indicate approximately the periods of church building by your observation of the main architectural features. If the church has a guide or plan displayed, you can use the details on your plan.

7 English parish churches are beautiful and their architecture is one of the treasures of our heritage. Pause to reflect on what is striking and pleasing about the details you are recording. You can perhaps realise the loving care, dedication and wealth that went into the building of the church by the community. Contrast this with the difficulties met with nowadays in these wealthier times, to maintain and restore the church.

8 From the major architectural features which give the overall appearance, impression and atmosphere of the church, we move on to the more detailed points. Examine and record carefully any of the following which are present.
a. font; b. piscina and sedilia; c. rood screen; d. evidence of rood loft and rood loft stairs; e. tombs, especially medieval ones with effigies; f. brasses; g. remains of wall paintings and doom painting; h. pieces of sculpture; i. roof lines; j. roof timbers and their carvings; k. stained glass; l. squint; m. aumbry; n. reredos. All of these and other similar features are worth recording for the way they help to fill in details of the church's history. Some give clues to church rebuilding (piscina, roof lines). Some illustrate the changing story of church development (rood loft, doom paintings). Some show how people lived (armour and clothing shown on tombs, brasses and carvings in wood and stone).

9 Special among these features is the furniture: seating, pulpit, lectern, choir stalls. See if you can find out when these date from and take particular note if the church has any very old examples of these items. Details of wood carving are most interesting and worth careful examination and recording.

10 With all these clues you are now in a position to work out an outline history of the church. What stages of general church development have left their impression on your church?

11 As well as being a record of general church history, the parish church offers details of the history of the local community. The oldest connections to be seen are usually with important families of the district. The tombs studied above for details of dress and armour tell us about them. In addition look for family chapels, family vaults and plaques. Local charities, lists of rectors or vicars, donors of stained glass windows are all pointers to stories from the past. Look for other associations as for instance with local regiments, or with events that took place nearby or, as in Melbourne Church, Derbyshire, the connection with Melbourne in Australia.

12 If arrangements are made beforehand, it may be possible for you to be shown the church plate and, if they are still kept at the church, the old registers. What is meant by 'church plate'? What is it used for? Who presented the church with its plate? Does it have any identifying marks? How far back do the registers date? What information is recorded in them? Why do historians find church registers particularly valuable?

13 Features of the churchyard:
a. How many entrances to the church-yard are there? Why were these particular positions chosen for entrances?
b. Is there a lych gate? Draw it. How old is it? State once again the purpose of the lych gate.
c. Count the evergreen trees. What type are they? Remember their significance.
d. What is the earliest gravestone you can find and the most recent? If burials no longer take place there what is the reason? Are there graves on the north side of the church? What are the main materials used for headstones? Do they vary according to date? Make rubbings of clear and interesting head-stones.

14 Imagine the church in use at different times during its history. Describe an occasion in the church at one of these periods. Bring into your account a description of the church as it appeared at the time.

10 Later Castles

After the Battle of Hastings, William the Conqueror granted the land of England to his most important followers who had to swear to be true to him and to give him service. Many of them were allowed to fortify their houses, or in other words, to build castles. These castles became the centres of law and order enabling the new landowners to keep Saxons under their control.

In the beginning, as we have seen in Chapter 6, they were made of earth and timber and were quickly built. As Norman control became firmer, the larger and more important castles were rebuilt in stone. This cut down the risk of fire, which was a constant danger in time of peace let alone in wartime. A few castles were actually built of stone right from the time of the Conquest.

At first these new castles followed the plan of the simple motte and bailey, but as the centuries passed, the defences became more and more complicated. This was necessary as the weapons of attack became stronger.

The castles were normally owned by the king or great barons but many belonged to important men in the Church, for the Church also held vast areas of land during the Middle Ages.

With the invention of gunpowder, however, the importance of castles was reduced and also, as life was becoming more peaceful, comfort began to be considered more important than fortification in the planning of buildings. By the fifteenth century the fortified manor house was replacing the castle, the usefulness of which was now almost at an end.

Norman Castles

During the twelfth century the wooden tower of a castle was often replaced by a stone curtain wall which had a range of living and store rooms inside it. Such a castle is called a shell keep. Soon, however, the building of strong square stone towers and thick outer walls around the bailey, meant that the mound for the keep was no longer so important. This is the sort of castle we often think of as typically Norman.

Use the information given to you in the drawing and write a description of a Norman castle. Find out what the inside of the keep was like and include a description of it in your writing.

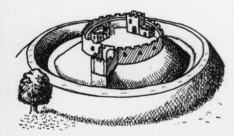

Above: a shell keep
Right: a Norman castle

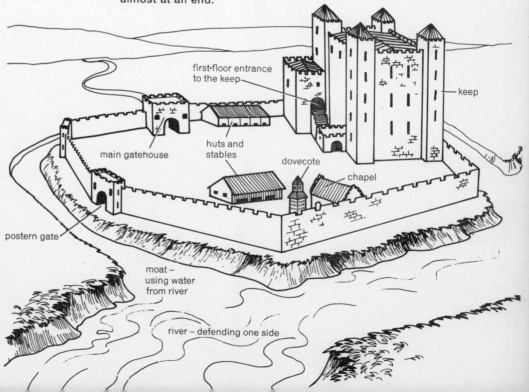

first-floor entrance to the keep

keep

main gatehouse

huts and stables

dovecote

chapel

postern gate

moat – using water from river

river – defending one side

The Growth of Castles

1 By the end of the twelfth century, men who had been fighting in the Crusades were bringing back to Europe completely new ideas in castle building. One of these ideas was the concentric castle. What does this mean? Why were the inner walls higher than the outer ones? Why did the keep become less and less important?

2 Why were round towers built instead of square ones? Flanking towers began to be constructed at intervals around the curtain walls. How did these strengthen the defences?

3 Where were the main living quarters placed in this sort of castle?

4 Some of the finest concentric castles of Britain are the castles of North Wales. When and why were they built? Draw up a list of the most important ones.

5 In your list you should have included Beaumaris on the Isle of Anglesey; locate this on a map of North Wales. Why was a castle needed here?

Beaumaris Castle

Compare the two pictures of Beaumaris.

1 It was built on flat marshy land. What natural feature became the strongest point in the defences? What has happened to this today?

2 Identify each of the following on both illustrations:

a. the gate next to the sea

b. the dock

c. the outer and inner curtain walls

d. the outer and inner wards

e. the many flanking towers

f. both gatehouses—which one was the main living area?

g. the town wall

h. Beaumaris

3 Show all these on a plan of the castle.

4 Explain how the town and the castle helped to defend each other.

5 Why were the gate next to the sea and the gatehouse not directly opposite each other?

6 Imagine you lived in Beaumaris when the castle was being built. Send a letter to a friend telling of the strength of this great building.

It is interesting to know that Beaumaris was never fully completed—perhaps even at that early date King Edward I realised that the importance of castles was declining.

Beaumaris Castle, Anglesey, as it would have looked when built

Beaumaris Castle as it is today

Attack and Defence

1 In the days before gunpowder, who had the hardest job—the attackers or the defenders of a castle? Think about this and write your answer when you have studied this section.

2 There were three ways in which a castle could be captured: by surprise attack, by siege or blockade, and by battery. Which would probably be the most successful? Why?

3 What would be the great advantage to the attackers if the castle could be taken by surprise?

4 The gate was always the weakest part and was elaborately defended. What do the following terms mean: *a*. moat; *b*. barbican; *c*. drawbridge; *d*. portcullis; *e*. machicolation; *f*. arrow loops; *g*. meurtrières or murder holes; *h*. pits? Copy the picture of the gatehouse and label each of these features.

5 What were the purposes of sally ports and postern gates?

6 The siege of a castle was often a long and weary business especially when it was strongly defended and well supplied. There was always the risk to the attackers of a relief force arriving to help the people in the castle. Siege weapons were therefore used. Many of these are illustrated in the drawing. Explain carefully what each one did.

7 What is meant by crenellating the castle walls? Why were hoardings sometimes built around the outside of the top of the walls? In later castles the walls were 'battered' to try to stop ramming. Explain with the help of a diagram what this means.

8 One means of attack was mining. This meant digging a tunnel under the castle wall and then setting fire to the timber supports of the tunnel. This caused the roof and the castle wall above to collapse. What were the ways of preventing a castle from being mined?

9 For many years, longbows and crossbows were the main personal weapons. Find out the difference between them. Which was the better weapon and why?

Stokesay Castle: a fortified manor house

This small, homely castle in Shropshire was far enough away from the Welsh border to enjoy the protection of its larger and more powerful neighbours—Ludlow and Shrewsbury. It was started early in the thirteenth century as a medieval house with a great hall and

A castle under attack

A castle gatehouse

outbuildings. In 1291 it was crenellated with a strong tower and defence walls. During Tudor times the gatehouse was added. Later in the seventeenth century a timbered north tower completed Stokesay as we see it today, a fine example of a fortified manor house.

Living in Castles

We must never forget that as well as being strong fortresses in times of war and law courts where wrongdoers were punished, castles were also homes, often for large numbers of people. In early times the castle was probably a cold, draughty, damp, dirty and crowded building, but as the centuries passed life became more comfortable. Study the life in a castle under the following topics.

1 *Inside the castle* furniture, tapestries and floor coverings, heating and lighting, windows (glass and shutters), the timbered and vaulted ceilings, decoration, staircases.

2 *The main rooms* the great hall, the kitchen, buttery and pantry, the bower and solar, the chapel, the armoury.

3 *People in the castle* their dress, work and wages. The lord and his family, knights and soldiers, ordinary servants, the chaplain, steward, castellan, falconer, farrier, fletcher, armourer, minstrels and chronicler.

4 *Daily life in the castle* gathering food and fuel supplies, keeping guard, making and repairing armour and weapons, games and pastimes, masques and tournaments, vigil, courtship and marriage, dowries, providing hospitality, administering justice, treatment of prisoners.

5 *Food and drink* supplies, menus, table manners, meat and spices, cellars and storehouses, dovecotes, brewhouses and bakehouses, water supplies.

6 *Sanitation* garderobes, refuse, smoke, smells, lack of privacy, stables and cattle sheds, disease.

Stokesay Castle, Shropshire

A Castle Study: Ashby-de-la-Zouch, Leicestershire

The Story of the Castle

The history of Ashby Castle began when William I granted the manor of Ascebi to one of his important followers, Hugh de Grentmaisnil. No doubt there was soon a plain wooden manor house built, probably in the grounds of the present castle. In the mid-twelfth century the estate passed to Alan la Zouch and at about this time the first stone buildings were erected. The remains of these form the outer walls of the present Great Hall.

As the family fortunes grew so did their house; a buttery and pantry were added in the thirteenth century, and a magnificent kitchen tower and a fine new solar in the fourteenth century.

During the troubled times of the Wars

The Hastings Tower, Ashby-de-la-Zouch Castle, Leicestershire

of the Roses the manor of Ashby returned to the Crown, until in 1464 Edward IV gave it to his Lord Chamberlain, William Lord Hastings. He was soon licensed to fortify the buildings and by adding a great tower, a chapel and other rooms and walls, he turned the old manor house into a castle.

For almost two hundred years Ashby was one of the most important homes in the Midlands, entertaining and sometimes imprisoning royalty. In the early seventeenth century a fine new suite of rooms was built to accommodate King James I.

During the Civil War it was a stronghold for Charles I and bravely withstood many attacks before being laid waste in 1649.

After being ravaged by the weather for three centuries, it is now in the care of the Department of the Environment.

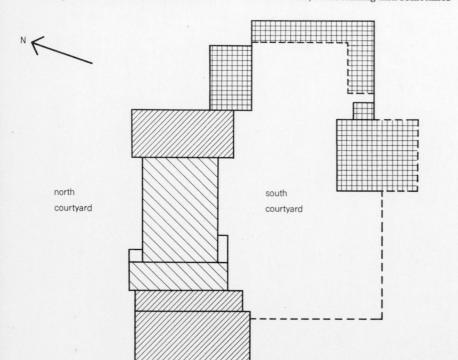

N

A plan of the main buildings of Ashby-de-la-Zouch Castle

north courtyard

south courtyard

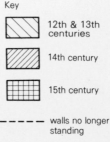

Key

▨	12th & 13th centuries
▨	14th century
▦	15th century
- - - -	walls no longer standing

1   Make your own copy of the plan of the castle. Using the outline history of Ashby, colour and name each block of the building. Explain by reference to the plan how the work of Lord Hastings turned the house into a castle.

2   What important castle features are missing from this plan?

3   The most important buildings represent several styles of architecture according to the time when they were built. Prepare a selection of the types of windows and doorways which you would expect to see in each part.

4   In places the castle walls are as much as eight feet thick: how were such walls made? What is the difference between rubble and dressed stone?

5   Like many of our castles, Ashby has ties with famous people and important events. Among these are the following:
a. William the Conqueror and the Domesday Survey
b. Edward IV and the Wars of the Roses
c. The Council of the North (the Earl of Huntingdon, the owner of Ashby, was its Lord President under Elizabeth I)
d. James I and Anne of Denmark who visited Ashby several times in the early seventeenth century
e. Mary Queen of Scots who was imprisoned here
f. Charles I, Prince Rupert and the Civil War
g. The Countess of Huntingdon and the evangelical movement of the eighteenth century
h. Sir Walter Scott and *Ivanhoe*
Imagine you lived at Ashby during the life of one of these people, and write an eye-witness account of how they affected the castle.

6   Study the photograph of the Hastings Tower. It is a fine example of a strong tower house and resembles the great keep of an early Norman castle. Write your own description of it mentioning such points as the building material, the doorways, the chimney-pieces, the windows, the machicolations. When and how was the tower reduced to its present ruined state?

7   Why is it important that our castles and other old buildings are preserved?

Fieldwork at a later castle

Castle visits can be both exciting and informative. To avoid missing anything of importance, fieldwork should be planned around the following main points while making full use of details as given in the various sections throughout this chapter.

1   *The site and the surroundings* Describe the position of the castle and give reasons why a castle was built here. Explain how the surroundings have changed. Note any connections between the castle and the local town or village.

2   *Type of castle and its development* Remember that most castles have grown over several centuries. Obtain a plan of the castle and study the remains of the different periods of the castle's growth.

3   *How the castle was defended—signs of attack* Look closely for all details of fortification such as the moat, gates, walls and towers.

4   *Domestic buildings and everyday life* Make a careful record of any remains, to show what living in the castle must have been like.

5   *Important events and famous people* associated with the history of the castle.

6   *The castle today* Its appearance and use. Who now owns and looks after the castle?

11 Enclosures

Enclosure meant the fencing, hedging or walling of individual pieces of land which had previously been part of open fields. There were two ways of enclosing the land, either by the common agreement of all the villagers or by an Act of Parliament.

Some Enclosure Features of an English Village

Key to drawing

1 Hedges around fairly rectangular fields give the distinctive pattern to the countryside.

2 Enclosed land that has been under grass for most of the time since enclosure still shows ridge and furrow—the remains of the strips in the former open fields.

3 The nucleus or village centre. Formerly all the houses of the village were here and most of these would have been farms. Among the many houses there are now usually only a few farms.

4 Farms away from the village centre were usually built after enclosure. The farmer now had all his land in one part of the village instead of in scattered strips.

5 Lanes going out from the village in all directions. Some are as old as the village. Many were made when the land was enclosed.

6 Right-angled bends in a country lane suggest the road might be very old. The medieval track went round blocks of strips in the open field and this pattern was kept after enclosure.

7 Wide verges along the lane. At the time of enclosure a wide piece of land was often left for the road and only a narrow strip was actually needed.

8 Cottages on the old common land. These were the homes of people who were sometimes allowed to keep them when the common was enclosed.

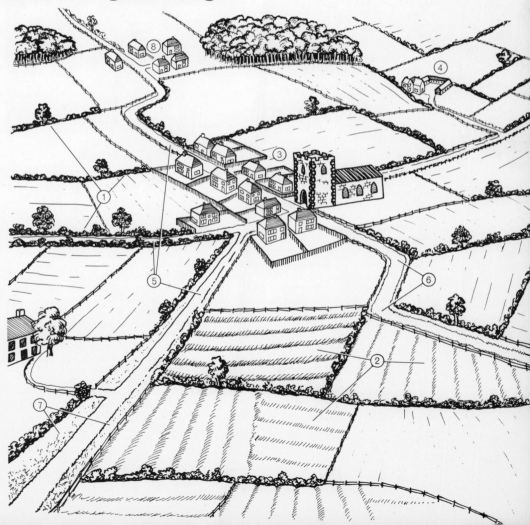

LONG MEADOW

SOUTH FIELD

MILL FIELD

Mill site

WEST FIELD

Open fields at Laxton, Nottinghamshire

7 Sykes are wide corridors of grassland in each field. The best remaining example is to be seen in the West Field across the bottom of the picture. What shows that this syke is low-lying land? Why was such a wide area not ploughed?

8 Baulks or unploughed strips were useful landmarks between holdings. Headlands allowed the oxen to turn at the end of a furrow. Both these were useful as paths to reach out-of-the-way strips. Examine the West Field carefully to find clear examples of baulks and headlands.

9 Draw a plan of the West Field showing as much detail as possible.

10 Was the mill a windmill or a watermill? Does the name of the field suggest it is a very old site? What was the importance of the mill to the village?

11 The curving ribbon of land next to the South Field was the Long Meadow. Why was the land near a stream used for meadow? How do the field boundaries in the Long Meadow give a clue to the way it was shared out in former times?

Fieldwork at an enclosure

1 If the village you are studying has an enclosure award, find out its date.

2 Find a place in the village with a good view over several fields. Draw a sketch of the fields and say what appearance they give to the landscape. What would the view have been like before the village was enclosed?

3 On the sketch, label the field boundary (hedge, wall, fence). Give details of the type of hedge or wall material. Say why this sort of field boundary was used.

4 Where enclosure took place gradually over the centuries, the field boundaries often followed the pattern of the old strips. With enclosure by Act of Parliament, the new fields usually did not follow the old pattern. Look for traces of ridge and furrow. Make sketch maps of what you find and say what they suggest about the type of enclosure.

Laxton Village and Open Fields

At Laxton in Nottinghamshire, parts of three medieval fields remain unenclosed and are still farmed on the open-field system. This is the nearest we can get today to see what a village was like before enclosure.

1 Why in a medieval village were all the farmhouses in the village centre?

2 Would you expect there to be more farms in Laxton now than in other village centres? Give reasons for your answer.

3 The long narrow fields to the left of the village street are the crofts of the medieval farms. What was their purpose? Why are they this shape? Find some which are made up of several narrower crofts. What does this tell you about the number of farms in the Middle Ages?

4 The single strips of former times have now been put into blocks. Explain why this is more convenient. Count the number of strips in some of the present-day holdings in the West field.

5 Each farmer has blocks of land in each open field. What are the drawbacks of farming in this way?

6 The crop rotation is as follows: *a.* wheat sown in the autumn; *b.* spring 'corn', that is any crop, even peas or beans, sown in the spring; *c.* fallow. Can you say what the crops of the three open fields were when the photograph was taken?

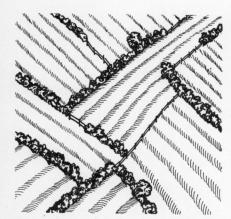

Fields where gradual enclosure has taken place following the former strip pattern

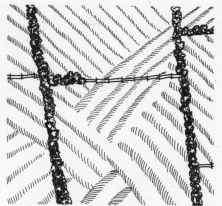

Fields where Parliamentary enclosure has taken place ignoring the former strip pattern

5 In many parts, modern farming methods are causing alterations in the field patterns as hedges are being removed to make larger fields. A careful study of the six-inch Ordnance Survey map will enable you to discover some of these changes. Why are these improvements being made? Why were the smaller fields regarded as improvements in the first place?

6 Look for examples of straight stretches of lane which might have been created by enclosure, and of medieval lanes with right-angled bends around former blocks of land.

7 Measure the width of a lane between hedges at various points. Is the width constant? How much is surface and how much is grass verge?

8 Visit an outlying farm. Draw the view of the farmhouse from the front. Does the style of architecture suggest when it was built? If several of these farmhouses can be visited, see if they appear to have been built about the same time.

9 Examine the farm buildings and decide which are the original buildings and which are later additions and alterations. Make a plan of the layout of the farm as it was when it was built.

10 Imagine you lived in the village at the time of enclosure. Write a conversation between several villagers giving arguments for and against enclosure.

A Georgian brick farmhouse

12 Battles

A visit to a battlefield means using a different sort of fieldwork, since we are looking at the scene of an historical event and not at the actual remains of the past. On such a visit a vivid imagination can really bring the scene alive, and details of the story of the battle are more easily understood and remembered.

The Battle of Naseby, 14 June 1645

The broken marshy ground lying between the Royalists and Roundheads north of the village of Naseby was not to the liking of either Prince Rupert or Cromwell, the rival cavalry commanders. Therefore both armies moved westward to take up positions facing each other across a shallow open vale called Broadmoor.

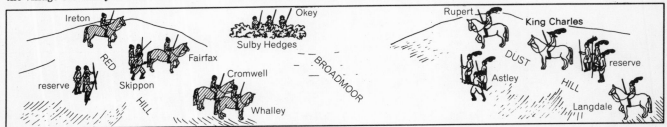

1   Parliament uses Red Hill Ridge as cover for their manoeuvres. Ireton faces Prince Rupert on the left; Cromwell has the cavalry on the right. Skippon commands the front part of the infantry, while Fairfax with the reserve infantry is the commander-in-chief. Colonel Okey with a thousand dragoons is sent behind Sulby Hedges on the far left flank.

On Dust Hill Ridge, Rupert has the cavalry on the Royalist right, Astley commands the infantry in the centre, while King Charles stays at the back with the reserve. Sir Marmaduke Langdale has the left-wing cavalry facing Cromwell.

2   The Royalists are outnumbered two-to-one but consider themselves better soldiers and attack. Rupert charges and defeats Ireton's cavalry. Royalist infantry advance in the centre and push back the Roundheads. Cromwell waits and watches Langdale's slow advance.

3 Rupert chases most of Ireton's cavalry from the field and attacks the Parliamentary baggage train at the rear.

When Langdale reaches the foot of the slope, Cromwell orders part of his cavalry under Colonel Whalley to charge.

Fairfax, seeing his infantry pressed back, sends in his large reserve.

4 The strength of the Parliamentary reserve gradually pushes back the Royalists in the centre. Cromwell charges from the right. Okey and the

remainder of Ireton's horse attack from the left.

Charles does not send in the Royalist reserve and retreats. Rupert returns to

the field only to see the defeat and then follows Charles northwards.

---

1 Draw a plan of the Battle of Naseby like the one given for the Battle of Bosworth (see next page). Draw blocks to show the positions of the armies at the start and arrows to show the movements which took place.

2 There was an important difference between the way the cavalry of the two sides fought during the Civil War. Find out what this difference was and say how this battle shows it.

3 Who do you think was the better commander, Sir Thomas Fairfax or King Charles?

4 As it happened, the charge of Colonel Okey's dragoons was important in winning the battle, but in what way were they placed in a dangerous position at the start?

5 From your research into the story of the Civil War say how important you

think this battle was in winning the war for the Roundheads.

Naseby Battlefield Today

Here is a view of Naseby field seen from Red Hill Ridge.

1 Which army would be on the ridge in the distance? Who commanded the cavalry on the left side of the ridge as you look at it?

2 The monument in the foreground commemorates Cromwell's decisive charge. It is thought to be wrongly placed too near the centre of the line. Which commander would view the field from the spot the photograph was taken?

3 Make a list of the differences in the

scene a soldier who fought in the battle would notice now.

The Battle of Bosworth

This is the way plans of battles are usually drawn, with blocks for the various armies and arrows to show the movement.

1 Look up the story of the Battle of Bosworth and use this plan to understand the details of what happened.

2 Which side appears to have had the best position at the start of the battle? Say why you think so.

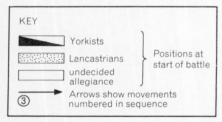

KEY

◣ Yorkists ⎫
▨ Lancastrians ⎬ Positions at start of battle
☐ undecided allegiance ⎭

③→ Arrows show movements numbered in sequence

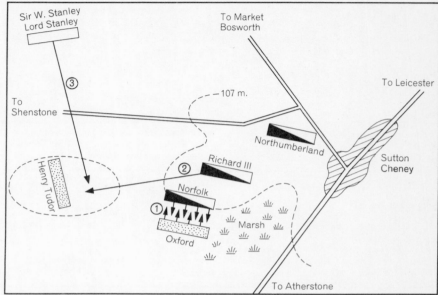

A plan to show the Battle of Bosworth

Fieldwork at a battlefield

a. Before the visit

1 During which war was this battle fought? Study the reasons why the war started.

2 Make a time chart of the events of the war.

3 Trace the movements of the armies just before the battle to find out how the battle positions were reached. Who chose the battleground? Did one side gain a better position than the other?

4 Go over the story of the battle in as much detail as possible. Make plans of the movements at different stages of the battle so that you can follow them on the ground.

5 Find out as much as you can about the leaders of both sides and other important people in the battle. What sort of men were they? What other great events were they associated with?

b. The visit

1 Examine the battlefield carefully and note the main features of the landscape which were important in the battle. Pay attention to such items as hills, valleys, slopes, uneven ground, rivers, streams, former marshes and heathlands.

2 Work out where each part of each army was at the start of the battle. Describe in detail the position of the various units. Give your opinions on the advantages and disadvantages of these positions.

3 The appearance of the countryside will have changed greatly since the battle. Make a list of the changes an observer of the battle would notice if he were here now.

4 From various positions on the battlefield trace the movements of the battle. Get to know where each important event in the battle took place.

5 Having done this, imagine the scene in the heat of battle. Tell the story as if you were one of the soldiers taking part. Or you can tell the story as a modern war correspondent might do for a newspaper.

6 What mistakes do you think were made by the side which lost the battle? In what different ways would you have fought the battle if you had been in command?

7 Sometimes there are relics of a battle to be seen nearby in churches or houses. Often there are memorials in the form of plaques or monuments. Make a detailed record of any of these in the area and list the names of fields, farms and roads which have associations with the battle.

8 In addition to these occasional relics, museums have displays of armour, dress and equipment, which were used at the time of the battle. A study of such equipment would help you understand the battle.

13 Parks and Country Houses

Every county has a number of country houses. Some are magnificent, such as Longleat in Wiltshire, others are small manors like Sulgrave in Northamptonshire. Whatever their size, they all form a valuable record of our social history and many are now open to the public to be visited and enjoyed.

Parks and Country Houses

To most people today, the word park means an open, green area of playing-fields, flower-beds and children's swings set in the middle of a busy town. Very few realise that a park used to be something very different from this.

In the Middle Ages parks were areas fenced off from the open countryside in which the local lords, by permission of the king, were allowed to keep herds of deer and in which hunting was restricted to the lord.

In later centuries, as their owners became richer and more important, these parks were often made larger and became the grounds of fine country houses.

New parks were also created around the large houses of the eighteenth century by fencing off areas of village farmland. In a few cases the whole village was destroyed or was moved elsewhere to make way for the park.

In more recent times local councils have been given the power by Act of Parliament to set aside land to be used as recreational parks. Many of these have a history well worth looking into.

Finally, in 1949 the Government began to choose areas of special beauty to be preserved as National Parks where everybody can enjoy the open country-side. These often extend over several hundred square miles.

The ruins of Bradgate House, Leicestershire

Bradgate Park and Ruins, Leicestershire

This is all that remains of one of the first unfortified great houses in England. The park, first mentioned in 1247, became the property of the Greys of nearby Groby Castle in the fifteenth century. In 1499 Thomas Grey, Marquis of Dorset, a wealthy and important man, began to build Bradgate House.

1 What was the name of the civil war fought in England during the second half of the fifteenth century? Edward IV married Elizabeth Woodville, the widow of Sir John Grey. What do you think was the effect of this marriage on the fortunes of the Grey family?

2 Why do you think Thomas Grey began to build this splendid mansion? What advantages would it have over his previous home?

3 What types of homes had the great

landowners lived in during the Middle Ages? Why? In what ways was Bradgate so different? Are there any signs of fortifications to be seen in the photograph?

4 What is the main building material shown? Why was this unusual for that time? How would it differ from the same material being used today? What type of windows can be seen? What is the shape of the high towers? Why did the house have to be so large?

5 Only one room remained more or less undamaged after a disastrous fire in 1694. This was the family chapel. Why do you think it is still kept in good repair?

6 Behind the tower in the foreground was a large tilting yard. What was this used for?

7 Read the story of Lady Jane Grey. Tell these events as if you were a servant at Bradgate in 1554 at the time of her execution. Legend has it that the heads of the great oaks in the park were cut off when news came to Bradgate of 'Queen' Jane's execution.

8 The park around the house is still very open and unspoilt—covered with bracken and with many rocky outcrops. What was such a large park used for? What is a deer leap? What does it look like? Why are the park fences still checked daily?

Fieldwork at a country house

1 *The outside of the building* Draw the front of the house. Label the chief features of the building. Find out the main style of architecture. Describe any ornamental features. Is there any part of the outside of the house not in keeping with the general effect? What are the main building materials used? Are they local? If not, where do they come from?

2 *The interior* Make a list of the main rooms in the house and explain the use of each. Contrast the principal rooms with the kitchens and the servants' quarters. Choose at least one room to describe in detail. Explain how the main services, such as lighting and heating, were provided for the house at the time when it was built, and how they are provided today. When you have been through the main rooms sum up in one sentence your impression of them. Draw a plan to show the layout of the inside of the house.

3 *Furniture and furnishings* Draw up a list of the names associated with the furnishings of the house, and explain why each is famous. Select samples of their fine craftsmanship to describe and sketch.

4 *People and events* Has the house any close associations with famous people or great historical events? Record briefly the history of the family which owned the property and any interesting stories told about them.

5 *The park and the garden* Discover how and when the park was created. Were any major changes made in the nature of the land when the house was built? Is there a deserted village site within the enclosure? Find the extent of the park and sketch the type of boundary wall. Have the grounds been specially landscaped? If so, describe the effect of this. Note any particular features such as a folly or an ornamental lake. Record the remains of any earlier buildings or earthworks in the park. List the main entrances and study the gatekeeper's lodge.

6 *The outbuildings* Survey the outbuildings of the house, describe the architecture and the uses of the buildings and discover what they are used for now. Visit the local parish church and record any connections with the house and its family.

7 Imagine you were associated with the house at an important period in its history. You might, for example be a member of the family, or a guest, or a servant. Write a diary of daily life in the house over a short period.

Constable Burton Hall, Yorkshire

Constable Hall is a magnificent house of the eighteenth century. This and earlier buildings have been the home of the Wyvill family for eight hundred years. Study the main features of the building and note how it differs from earlier and later architectural styles. Make your own collection of illustrations of different houses.

14 Turnpike Roads

The hundred years from 1750 to 1850 are known as the Industrial Revolution, when great changes took place in industry and farming. These changes made better transport essential. The improvements in transport came in three stages: roads and canals, then railways. The first of these improvements were the turnpike roads.

1   What happened to the roads in Britain when the Romans left?

2   What did the Statute of Winchester, passed in 1285, say? Why was there little need for good roads during the Middle Ages? What were chantry bridges?

3   The increase of trade in Tudor times led to more interest in improving the road system. What did the first Highway Act of 1555 order? Why was this Act unpopular?

4   When this failed to solve the problems of the roads, further Acts of Parliament were enforced during the reign of Charles II. What did these say? What was the purpose of the 'Broadwheel' Acts?

5   The Jacobite rebellions of 1715 and 1745 made the government realise that good roads were necessary. What did they do about it?

6   Why did the Industrial Revolution bring an increased demand for better transport? What was the Turnpike Trust system? What weaknesses did the system have? What were the names of the great road-builders of this period?

7   Why did roads become less important during the nineteenth century?

8   What happened to the turnpike trusts during the latter half of the nineteenth century? How are roads now classified? Who is responsible for maintaining each class of road? Why are tolls still charged on certain roads and bridges?

Tollgates

1   Who built these toll houses? On which roads were they constructed? Explain fully the work of the man who lived in the toll house.

2   Describe the construction of the building. What is unusual about the shape of the front of the house? Explain carefully why it would be built in this way. Who would use the verandahs?

3   Why would people study the board which was usually placed at the side of the gate or on the front of the toll house?

Kennington Turnpike Gate

Find details of the likely charges made. What would be the effect of these charges on the cost of travel? What was the difference between a turnpike and a tollgate? Is there a tollgate in your area?

4   How is this road surfaced? Such roads were hard-wearing but rather bumpy. What were many country roads like at that time? What is the roadman doing? How long ago do you think this picture was made? The dress of the people and the gas lamps should help you decide. In what ways is this scene likely to have changed by today?

Fieldwork at a turnpike road

1   Find out which of your local roads were turnpikes. What were the names of the trusts responsible for them?

2   Do any of the old toll houses remain? How far apart were they built generally? Why have many toll houses disappeared in recent years?

3   Visit a toll house. Draw plans and and sketches and note any alterations which have been made to the building since it ceased to be a toll house.

4   Are there any names, such as 'bar' or 'gate' which indicate the former existence of toll houses?

5   Explain why very few stretches of turnpike road exist in their original state. If any do remain, record details of the width and construction of the turnpike road.

6   Draw a sketch map of your area and mark on it as many of the above points as you can.

The Old Blue Boar, Holborn

A Coaching Inn

1   How did the name stage-coach originate? With the building of better roads came the era of the stage-coach. What years did this cover? By the year 1800 what was the average speed for a coach?

2   Find out as much as you can about the construction of stage-coaches. Where did the passengers ride? Which were the most expensive seats? What materials were used? How were they sprung?

3   What government action was taken in 1784 to increase the importance of coach travel? How did the mail coaches warn the tollgate-keepers of their approach?

4   What were the two main functions of coaching inns? Study the picture and describe the building. Why was the coach office important? Why was the clock in such a prominent position? Why were these inns usually built around a courtyard? Where would the archways lead you?

5   What are the names of the two vehicles that you can see? What other type of coaches would you have seen on the roads in these days?

6   What would have been the work of each of the following: *a.* the ostler; *b.* the postilion; *c.* the landlord; *d.* the groom? Why would speed be essential in their work?

7   Why is the traditional romantic idea of stage-coach travel probably very far from the truth?

Fieldwork at a coaching inn

Many coaching inns can still be found with remains of the yard and former stables.

1   Study the inn yard carefully and note the structure of the building, including such details as the yard, the archway, remains of lamp brackets, the stables and rooms for the many employees.

2   Draw and label the yard and buildings as they used to be.

3   What are the present uses of these buildings? Are any of them still connected with transport?

4   On what main road was this inn in coaching days? Is the inn more or less important than it used to be? Account for any changes.

5   Are there any relics of coaching days inside the inn? Record any interesting information which they tell you about the former days of the inn.

15 Canals

Canal building was the second stage of the revolution in transport. Horses could haul many more times the weight of cargo if it was afloat than if it had to be carried by land. Thus the canals enabled the heavy materials for the growing industries to be moved about easily. Most of our canals were built between 1760 and 1800 and many of them are still in use and can readily be studied.

Some features to look for along canals

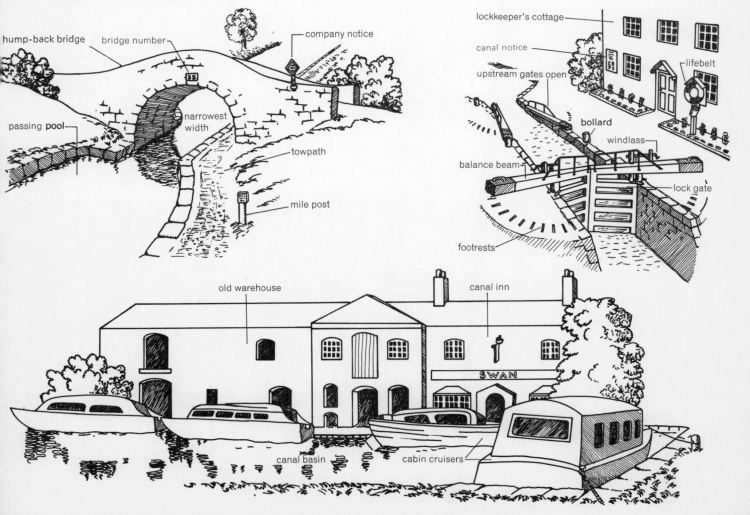

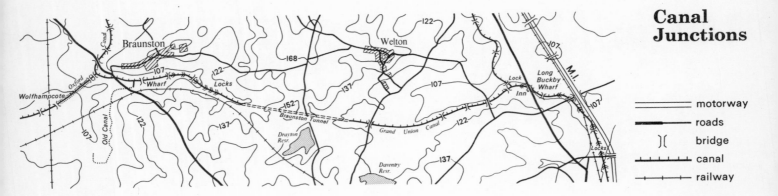

Canal Junctions

Legend:
- motorway
- roads
- bridge
- canal
- railway

Here is a map showing where the Grand Union Canal joins the Oxford Canal on the borders of Northamptonshire and Warwickshire, a few miles south of Rugby.

1 Find out when these canals were built and who were the engineers in charge.

2 From a detailed map of canals in Britain say which places these canals lead to.

3 Make a tracing of the map showing contours and canals. Shade in the land over 122 metres. Say how the shape of the land influenced the course of the canals.

4 Give three different methods used by the canal builders to overcome changes in the height of the land along the chosen route. Show them on your tracing.

5 The Grand Union Canal is a summit canal. What does this mean?

6 Most of the bridges over the canal carry well-marked roads and railways but some, like the one north of Braunston at the top of the map, are shown with no roads at all. Count how many such bridges there are. Why do you think they were built?

7 Suggest reasons for the wharves at Long Buckby and Braunston.

8 How old do you think the inn at Long Buckby is?

The canal basins at Stourport

Stourport

Stourport is a rare example of a town created by canals. Before the building of this inland port about two hundred years ago there were no houses here.

1   What river is shown in the front of the photograph? Notice the width of this waterway and the ease of navigation along it.

2   Which canal joins the river here? Notice its course from the right of the canal basin to the top centre of the photograph. Where does this canal lead to?

3   Why were such large canal basins built? Why do they have such prominent right-angled bays?

4   Examine carefully the two ways of reaching the canal basin from the river. Why is one wider than the other? How many locks are there to each route?

5   The basin nearest to the bridge over the river does not connect with the canal. What was its purpose?

6   What evidence is there of industry connected with the canal port?

7   The great trading days of the port are over but the waterways are still active. Give details of the present-day uses of them as shown in the photograph.

8   Most of the features around the canal basin are Georgian. Why should most of the houses in Stourport be of this period?

9   The large hotel facing the river to the right of the photograph was one of the first buildings erected in Stourport. What sort of people would have used it at the end of the eighteenth century?

Fieldwork at a canal

Study a two- or three-mile section of a canal in groups, with the work divided between individuals. Study an even longer stretch if you can. A careful study of the Ordnance Survey map before setting out is helpful in understanding why the particular route was chosen for the canal.

1   Measure the width of the canal at various points. What is its average width? What is the narrowest width you record? Where does it occur? What type of boats could use the canal?

2   In the case of disused canals where the bed is dry, estimate the average depth. How did the engineer keep the water in the canal?

3   How do canals lose water? Record any means of supplying water to the canal.

4   As you proceed along the canal observe carefully its exact course. Account for the choice of this route in every detail.

5   How were obstacles to the course of the canal overcome? Record details of locks, cuttings, embankments, tunnels and aqueducts.

6   Note down every building associated with the canal. In each case say what purpose it served. Is the building now used for something else? Have these canal buildings any architectural features in common?

7   Are there any clues to the cargo the canal carried?

8   What was the reason for building any side-branch of the canal?

9   Record any evidence of tramways bringing cargoes to the canal. What materials were carried by the tramway?

Why was this particular form of transport used?

10   Why are canal bridges attractive to look at? Draw or photograph examples. Why are there so many bridges?

11   Notice the numbering of the bridges. If any numbers have gone, locate the site of the missing bridge. What was the original reason for building this bridge? Why do canals narrow at the bridge?

12   Look for and record interesting canal notices. What do they tell you about the history of the canal?

13   Account for any specially wide stretches of canal.

14   Look for and record canal mileposts.

15   Look out for any of the following along the canal: sideposts, stopgates, staunches, roving bridges. What were they used for?

16   Imagine the canal being built by gangs of navvies: the bustle, the noise, the disturbance. How would these hundreds of men be organised? How would they be fed? Where would they sleep? Would the local people be pleased to have the navvies in the neighbourhood? Which people would benefit most by their presence?

17   Draw a general view of the canal and label on it as much information as possible.

18   List the present-day uses of the canal.

16 Railways

When you hear the word railways you probably picture huge giants of iron and steel busy on their journeys through town and countryside. Few people stop to think that a railway consists of two parts, the track itself as well as the train. Laid tracks had been used for many centuries before the engine was invented in the early nineteenth century. The combination of track and engine was one of the greatest steps in the history of transport.

1   In the seventeenth and eighteenth centuries these tracks were called tramways or wagonways. What important industry used them most? What were the tracks made from? What was the importance to the tramway owners of new, cheap ways of making iron?

2   Explain briefly the parts played by Thomas Newcomen and James Watt in the story of steam power.

3   What was strange about the steam locomotives of Nicholas Cugnot and Richard Trevithick? What was the idea behind the 'rack' locomotive?

4   George Stephenson's name is the most famous in railway history. What are the two railway lines in the north of England built by Stephenson between 1825 and 1830?

5   What advantages had railways over other forms of transport?

6   Why is it often said that during the middle years of the nineteenth century the country went railway-mad?

7   Why were the following Acts of Parliament important?
a. The Cheap Trains Act, 1844
b. The Railway Companies Act, 1921
c. The Nationalisation Act, 1947

8   What great changes have been made over the last twenty years in our railways? What part did Dr Beeching play in these changes? Do you think railways will disappear altogether in the future?

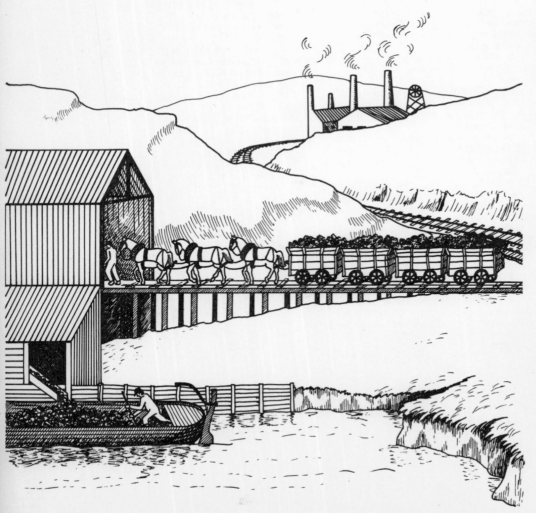

An early wagonway

Some Early Railways in the East Midlands

This is a sketch map of parts of Leicestershire, Derbyshire and Nottinghamshire showing some of the railways and canals which were built during the Industrial Revolution.

1 What important industries were growing in Leicester, Loughborough, Nottingham and Mansfield towards the end of the eighteenth century?

2 With the invention of the steam engine and the growing need for it to drive the factory machines, coal became a vital commodity. Where would the coal for these places come from? Before canals and railways were built, how would it have been transported?

3 Even before the Industrial Revolution the river Trent was an important navigable waterway. What does this mean?

4 In 1777 a canal was built down the Erewash Valley to bring coal to the Trent. Why do you think it was not continued to Mansfield as was first planned?

5 A tramway was built instead from Pinxton Wharf to Portland Wharf in Mansfield. What were the trucks like on these early tramways? How were they first pulled along? How was this improved by the use of stationary steam engines?

6 This particular line was not opened until 1819 owing to a dispute over the best sort of rails to use: plate rails or fish-bellied edge rails. What was the difference between them? The latter were eventually used here.

7 Imagine the scene at Pinxton Wharf in 1821: the tramway trucks, the barges, the hustle and the noise; the ponies, navvies, mounds of coal and limestone. A popular pub was here and several terraces of workers' cottages. Describe the picture as vividly as possible.

8 During the years 1776–93 the river Soar was made navigable from the Trent to Leicester. What would be done

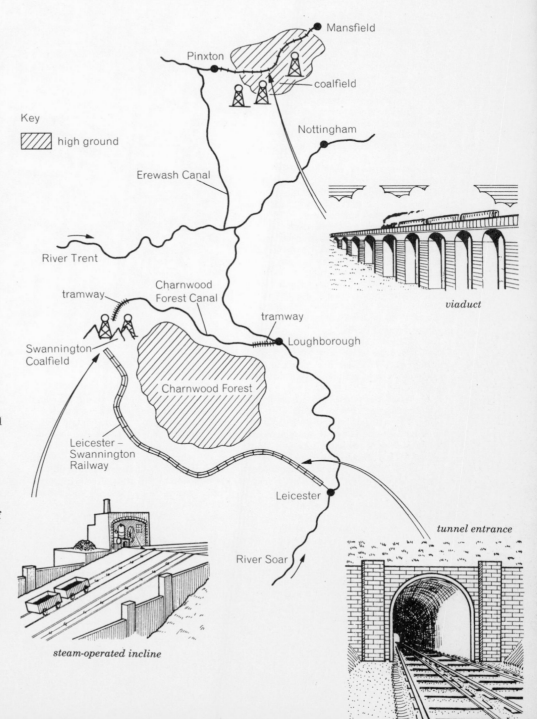

Key

 high ground

Mansfield

Pinxton

coalfield

Nottingham

Erewash Canal

River Trent

viaduct

tramway

Charnwood Forest Canal

tramway

Loughborough

Swannington Coalfield

Charnwood Forest

Leicester – Swannington Railway

Leicester

tunnel entrance

River Soar

steam-operated incline

to the river? This enabled coal to arrive in Leicester from the Nottinghamshire pits at 2½p per 50 kg. Trace the route of these coal barges. Why would it be a three-day journey? Why did the Leicestershire mine-owners object to this cheap Nottinghamshire coal?

9 The Charnwood Forest Canal with tramways at either end was built to enable them to compete but it was a disastrous failure. Does the map indicate why?

10 Thirty years went by until the problem of the transport of Leicestershire coal was solved. Why did local mine-owners go north to see George Stephenson about this problem in 1828?

11 Stephenson and his son Robert planned the route of the Leicester-Swannington Railway which opened in 1832. How did the local geography influence the route taken by the railway?

12 Who had to give permission before the railway promoters could actually begin to build a line? Which groups of people often violently objected to railways being built?

13 Why did early railways such as these two have to be built level or have only very slight gradients? Explain the different ways of achieving this shown in the sketches.

14 What problems were caused by the gauge of railways before 1846?

15 You will notice that both these railways were built by private companies. This was true of railways all over Britain. What were the drawbacks to this? What advantages should we have had if one firm, or the government, had organised the system from the start?

Both these lines were owned by the Midland Railway Company, later by the LMS and now, of course, by British Rail. Thus their history illustrates the story of railways in Britain.

Fieldwork at a disused railway station

1 On what line is the railway station? Where did it come from and go to?

Seaton Station, Rutland

Which company did it belong to? Has it closed down completely or is it still used for any goods traffic? When was the line built? Were there any special reasons behind its building?

2 Which village or villages did the station serve? What is the present population of the area? Has it changed greatly in recent years? Do you think this would ever have been a busy passenger station? Why would the passengers use the railway?

3 What goods would have been handled? Are there any particular places where these would have been sent? Are there any remains showing how this was done? Look particularly for such things as coal wharves, warehouses, loading platforms and grain silos. Make a careful record of them.

4 Show the layout of the whole site with all the lines and buildings. Record any sidings, junctions, signal boxes, platforms, crossing gates and bridges.

5 Draw a plan of the station. Show all the rooms and account for their use.

6 Describe the structure of the buildings; were they built of local materials? How were they lit? How were they heated? Are there any interesting architectural details? Record any dates you find on the buildings.

7 When was the station last used both for goods and for passenger traffic? Why have such stations fallen into disuse in recent years? Were there any special reasons why this one closed? What alternative means of transport are now available for the local trade and former passengers?

17 A Village Study

Every village contains remains of its history over the centuries, and is a worthwhile subject for fieldwork. This is best undertaken as a group project, but it can be tackled by one person working over a longer period.

Such fieldwork is the recording and understanding of historical remains. It is not meant to be a parish history, which can only be written from a study of many documents. However, if any documents are available, they can help and you will find old maps, such as the enclosure award or nineteenth-century tithe map, especially useful to trace boundaries, field patterns and roads and to establish the date and purpose of buildings.

Many of the topics which can be presented in a village study have already been dealt with in this book. The next few pages cover some additional material.

Parish Boundaries

Where they have not been changed in recent times, the parish boundaries are often among the oldest relics of the village and are fascinating to explore.

In the first place only a tiny amount of land was farmed around the village and for most of their length the boundaries were in the uncleared forest or waste. To avoid endless disputes, clear boundaries which everyone could recognise were essential.

Study the boundaries of your parish on large-scale Ordnance Survey maps and then explore them on foot, observing their special features.

1 Which lengths of boundary follow or make use of natural features such as rivers, streams, ridge and hilltops?

2 Where do boundaries follow man-made features such as roads, tracks, sunken lanes and hedges? Sometimes these features are of great antiquity. Can you estimate or find out how old they are?

3 Although they are rare nowadays, look for boundary stones, boundary posts and other similar marks. When were they erected?

4 On a sketch map of the boundaries of the village, indicate all the natural and man-made features.

5 Explain, as far as you can, the choice of boundaries.

6 Why was the ceremony of 'Beating the Bounds' at Rogationtide so important in the Middle Ages? Imagine you took part. Write the day's diary of events.

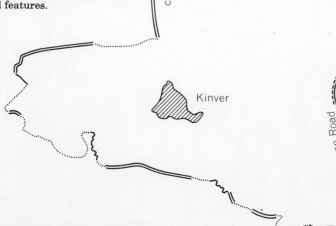

Boundaries of the parish of Kinver, Staffordshire

Key	
··············	parish boundary
∿∿∿	along streams
═══	along roads and tracks
− − − −	along ridges

Village Sites

When villages were set up, their first inhabitants chose the sites with care. A study of the position of the village will often reveal the reasons why that particular spot was chosen.

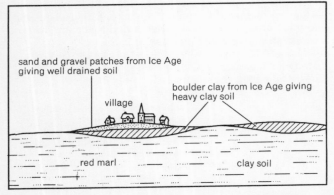

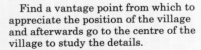

A village built on a dry site among the clay soils of the Midlands.

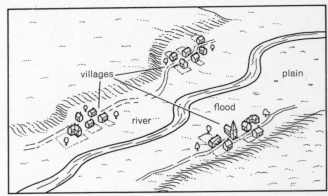

Villages built on the edge of lowland sometimes flooded by the river

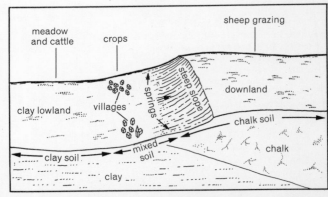

Spring line villages at the foot of steep chalk slopes in southeast England

Find a vantage point from which to appreciate the position of the village and afterwards go to the centre of the village to study the details.

Here are some points to look for:

a. Nearness to water supply: by rivers, streams and springs

b. Routeways: such as valleys followed by the settlers moving inland along rivers and streams

c. Well-drained places: patches of gravel along rivers and in clay country, the edge of the fen, the edge of a river flood plain, slight rises in otherwise badly drained land

d. The junction of two different types of landscape: the foot of a ridge or where two types of rock come together. Such places offered variety in soils and land to the first villagers.

e. Shelter from wind and bad weather: hollows in slopes or below the crests of hills and ridges

f. Mining villages near deposits of coal and other minerals

Study Ordnance Survey maps for clues; it will also help to consider the position of nearby villages. Often similar sites were chosen in the same area.

Houses

Houses are of different shapes, sizes and ages and tell us a lot about the history of the village. To really learn about houses you must look at them very carefully. Here is a useful sheet which can be copied to be filled in for each house studied by the group.

Having collected the information, make an illustrated account of houses in the village. Compare the houses of different types, of different sizes, of different periods and try to explain the reasons for each type of building. What can the houses tell you about the social history of the village?

Sheet for recording details of a house in a housing survey

Address:
to ensure that the exact location of the house is known for future reference

Guttering, drainage:
materials used: iron, lead, asbestos, plastic, wood; any special feature or ornamentation

Windows (upper):
wood, metal, stone frames; design of frame, method of opening; number of panes; any significant alteration

Windows (lower):
details as above; any significant difference

Door and doorway:
details of doorway and any other clues to period

Other points of special interest

Type of house:
detached/semi-detached/ terraced/ bungalow etc.

Date of house or period:
known or estimated; if estimated, give reason for estimation

Roof: materials:
slate, tile, thatch, etc.; details about style of building e.g. shorter slates on top; details of chimney

Construction:
main style and type of construction; half-timber, brick, clapperboard, cruck frame etc. Include all relevant details such as type of brickwork, methods of hanging tiles, type of timber frame etc. If house is plastered, is it traditional design? What is it plastered over?

Foundations:
are the first few feet above the ground different from the rest of the house? e.g. wood or brick on stone base. Give details.

The Chapel

Most villages have at least one chapel. The religious history of the village can be traced through a study of its chapels, especially through those of the seventeenth century onwards. Since that date various groups have broken away from the Church of England. They were first called 'dissenters' and later 'non-conformists'. The division of non-conformists into various groups or sects is seen in the many chapels possessed by the larger villages.

Right: the interior of a large Methodist chapel

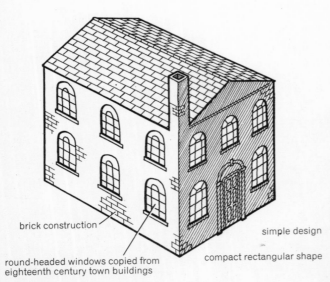

plastered walls

door to other schoolrooms and assembly rooms

pine board surrounds

organ

choir

gallery

memorial plaque

pulpit

communion table

iron supports for gallery

carpeted floor

pulpit and communion table removed and scaffolding and seating arranged for anniversary and performance of *The Messiah*

brick construction

simple design

compact rectangular shape

round-headed windows copied from eighteenth century town buildings

The exterior of a small Baptist chapel

Fieldwork at a village chapel

1   When was the chapel built? To which non-conformist group does it belong?

2   Study carefully and record the architecture both inside and outside the building. Take special note of the features illustrated in the diagram.

3   Make a scale plan of the chapel. Show the position of the seating, pulpit, gallery and other fixed items inside the chapel.

4   Where there is more than one chapel compare them with each other. What features have they in common? Why should this be so? Find out the differences in belief and worship between the various sects using the chapels.

5   In what ways is the chapel built differently from a church? Why?

6   Give the present-day use of any abandoned or converted chapels.

7   By asking older people, find out how much more important the church and chapels were in the social life of the village forty or fifty years ago than today.

54

The Village Plan

A large map of the village can serve as a central point for the display of your studies. The position of the historical remains can be shown on it with illustrations or written work arranged around it.

The village illustrated here shows the wealth of historical detail which can be studied and recorded. Ibstock, it is true, is a large village and an industrial one, but even small villages have a surprising number of historical features to record. One value of using Ibstock as an illustration is that on the surface it is most uninteresting and drab and it is certainly in no way picturesque. But once you probe more deeply all sorts of interesting points emerge.

A further use of the plan can be to show the stages of growth of the village. This is done by studying the dates of the houses and buildings.

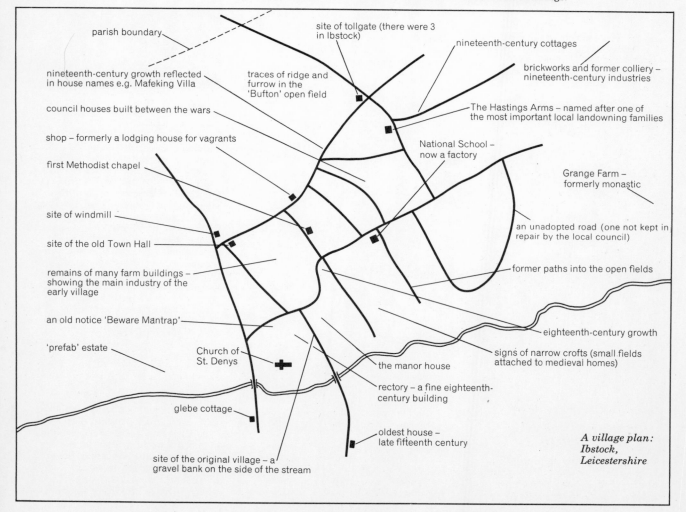

parish boundary

site of tollgate (there were 3 in Ibstock)

nineteenth-century cottages

brickworks and former colliery – nineteenth-century industries

nineteenth-century growth reflected in house names e.g. Mafeking Villa

traces of ridge and furrow in the 'Bufton' open field

The Hastings Arms – named after one of the most important local landowning families

council houses built between the wars

National School – now a factory

shop – formerly a lodging house for vagrants

Grange Farm – formerly monastic

first Methodist chapel

an unadopted road (one not kept in repair by the local council)

site of windmill

site of the old Town Hall

former paths into the open fields

remains of many farm buildings – showing the main industry of the early village

eighteenth-century growth

an old notice 'Beware Mantrap'

signs of narrow crofts (small fields attached to medieval homes)

'prefab' estate

Church of St. Denys

the manor house

rectory – a fine eighteenth-century building

glebe cottage

oldest house – late fifteenth century

site of the original village – a gravel bank on the side of the stream

A village plan: Ibstock, Leicestershire

Village Industries

Most villages show some signs of industrial activity. Visit and record all industrial remains and premises, including old machinery and equipment.

1 Look for rural crafts and industries such as the smithy, woodyard or mill. If the mill site is known, give the reason for its position.

2 Extractive industries such as iron mining, brick-making and quarrying leave clear signs of where they were carried out.

3 In coal-mining districts record, with dates, all former mines and present-day collieries. In particular look for the remains of early bell-pits which are occasionally to be found as mounds on the surface.

4 Look for houses which have indications they were used for domestic industry, like this cottage in Calverton, Nottinghamshire, which was used for framework knitting.

5 With present-day industries, find out when they started and the reason why they are in the village.

6 Use your findings to tell the story of industry in the village.

Other points of interest

Villages also contain an abundance of other historical remains. Such items as pumps, wells, beehives, dovecotes, stocks, lock-ups and market crosses each tell a part of the story of the village. It is often the smaller details which appeal to the imagination and hold the most fascination, whether it be an eighteenth-century fire mark, a thirty-year-old advertisement, or the 'VR' on the oldest post-boxes. Keep your eyes open for these relics, large and small, find out their meaning and importance, and make as comprehensive a list of them as you can. Imagine the village when each item was first used, and the difference it made to the life of the village.

Above: framework knitters' cottages at Calverton, Nottinghamshire

Left: the market cross at East Hagbourne, Berkshire

18 A Town Study

The Town Site

Find out why a town grew up in this precise spot. A careful study of the Ordnance Survey map should give you some clues.

Look especially for any connection of the town with a river, for many towns grew up by rivers. Could small boats use the river for transport? Was it a convenient crossing-place where a bridge could be built or the river forded? Is the town on a dry site in the valley? Did the river help in the town's defences? Would roads and tracks have followed the valley?

Is the town placed in a central position for trade, with easy routes in several directions?

When you are sure of the features of the town site, go to the town centre and, among all the buildings and activity, see if the factors originally governing the choice of the site can still be seen today.

The town, like the village, is best studied by a group. The difficulty of size can be overcome either by taking topics such as the town's development during a specific period in history, or by looking at a small part of the town, for instance housing, and studying its development through the ages.

Maps showing what the town was like at different times in the past are most helpful. This is especially true of a map giving the layout of the town in the Middle Ages. In addition, drawings and prints often show buildings as they used to be and printed guides and pamphlets to important places such as a castle or cathedral are sometimes available.

Visit museums for relics of the town's past and use these to add detail to the story.

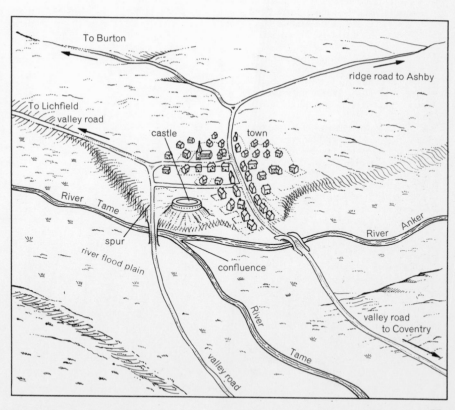

The site of Tamworth, Staffordshire

The Roman Town

Most of our towns and cities were founded long after Roman times. In those that are Roman in origin, there are usually only a few remains to be seen of the original town, because of the rebuilding which has taken place so many times on the same spot. Fieldwork on Roman towns may be difficult but two things can be aimed at. First build up a general picture of the Roman town and then pay close attention to what can be learned about the details of Roman life.

1 Study any fragments of building that are standing. What can you learn about Roman building methods? How were walls constructed? What materials were used? Describe Roman bricks and tiles. Where did the stone come from? Can any architectural details still be seen?

2 Parts of the Roman town may have been excavated and in some places the excavations are left open to view and preserved. In such cases make a plan of the remains and work out what each part was used for.

3 Of the chief features of a Roman town—walls, gates, basilica, forum, public baths, temple, amphitheatre—choose the one with the most substantial remains and imagine it being built. Make sketches and plans such as the builder might have used.

4 Parts of Roman buildings which are illustrated and described in your history books for their importance—baths, hypocausts, mosaic floors—can sometimes be seen first-hand. Where this is so, draw what you see and write about how it was made and used.

5 Draw a plan of the Roman town like the one shown for Cirencester. On it mark in separate colours: a. what Roman remains are still to be seen; b. what remains are known to exist through excavations, even though they have been covered up again; c. what can be worked out about the position of other streets, walls and gates.

6 Possibly the most interesting details of Roman times are to be seen in the objects of everyday life found by archaeologists and displayed in museums. Choose one aspect of Roman life to study and write about in detail.

A plan of Roman Cirencester (Corinium)

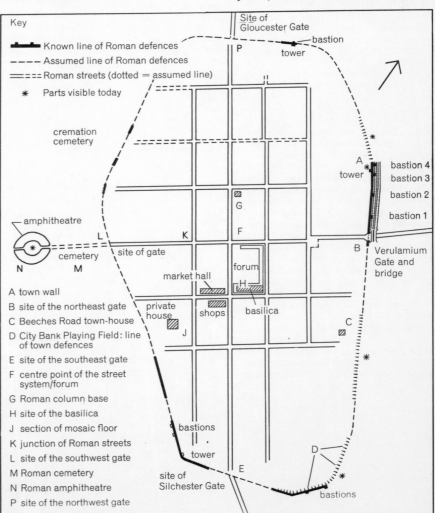

Key

— Known line of Roman defences
- - - Assumed line of Roman defences
==== Roman streets (dotted = assumed line)
* Parts visible today

A town wall
B site of the northeast gate
C Beeches Road town-house
D City Bank Playing Field: line of town defences
E site of the southeast gate
F centre point of the street system/forum
G Roman column base
H site of the basilica
J section of mosaic floor
K junction of Roman streets
L site of the southwest gate
M Roman cemetery
N Roman amphitheatre
P site of the northwest gate

The Medieval Town

1   Obtain, if possible, a map which shows the town as it was in the Middle Ages.

2   Make a tour of the perimeter of the medieval town in order to appreciate the size and extent of the town in the Middle Ages. Notice that the walk will probably only take you about half an hour. If the town had walls, record any remains. Find out what archaeologists have discovered about the height and thickness of the walls and the gates in them. Why were town walls considered necessary?

3   Compare the map of the medieval town with the present-day map. Walk through all the known medieval streets to get the 'feel' of them and of the street pattern. Note the narrowness of the streets which were once, perhaps, even narrower.

Look for street names giving the trades which were carried on there and names with other associations, such as '-gate' and '-mill'. Has the centre of the town shifted since the Middle Ages or are the main streets of that time the main shopping streets of today?

4   What exists of the sites of the market and fairs of the Middle Ages? Street names should help here. Describe and, if possible, explain the position of the market place and sites of fairs in the medieval town.

5   Is there a market cross? What was it for? If there is a market hall, when does it date from? When was the first market hall built? Does the market street widen to make room for the stalls or is there a definite square? Are there any blocks of later buildings filling up part of the old market place? On which day or days of the week is the market held? Since when have these days been traditional?

6   Explain the difference between markets and fairs and say why each was important. Is a fair still held? How did it begin? How has it changed since medieval times?

7   Churches should be studied in the way described for the parish church in Chapter 9. Find out how many churches existed in the medieval town and account for their number. How many are left and how large are their parishes? Study any monastic remains (see Chapter 8). Look for references to former monastic sites in street names such as Black Friars and Abbey Street.

8   If you are in a cathedral town, study the cathedral in the same way as suggested for the parish church but on a larger scale. In addition, other buildings associated with the cathedral will need to be recorded. Above all pay particular attention to important historical associations which the cathedral may have. For instance, Lincoln Cathedral has a copy of Magna Carta.

9   Is there a medieval guild hall in the town? What were guilds? How important were the merchant guilds and the craft guilds to the town? What business was transacted in a guild hall? Why did the guild hall sometimes become a town hall?

10   Where was the site of the medieval town hall? Does the building still exist? How would it compare with other buildings of the town in the Middle Ages? What business was carried on here? How did towns gain the right to control their own affairs?

Draw or photograph and describe these buildings and record any historical relics in them. What is the present-day use of the buildings?

Medieval Chester

Build up your own map of part of medieval Chester based on the photograph of Chester today (overleaf) and using these outline notes.

1   The City of Chester is one of the few English towns which still has its entire circuit of medieval wall. This follows, for much of its length, the wall of the Roman fortress of Deva. You can trace the wall here from the bottom right-hand corner of the photograph along the east and north side of the Cathedral Close.

2   This will also enable you to mark the position of the East and North Gates of the old city where the main streets reached the wall. The other two ancient gates were Bridgegate and Watergate. Both of these led to the river Dee and indicate Chester's early days as an important port.

3   The original market place was where Northgate Street widens opposite the west end of the cathedral. The present Market Hall and the Town Hall with its tower can be clearly seen there side by side on the west side of the Market Place.

4   In the Middle Ages the present cathedral was the church of the great monastery of St Werburgh—a Saxon princess. The buildings and their grounds covered much of the northeast quarter of the town before being destroyed by Henry VIII in 1540. The king allowed the citizens to keep the church as their cathedral.

5   There was little other open space left within the city wall and, as in most medieval towns, the houses and shops were closely packed together without much planning. Many of these old timbered buildings stiil remain, both in the street fronts and in the maze of alleys and narrow passages behind.

6   The main streets of Chester—the famous Rows—still follow the lines of the Roman streets. Northgate Street and its continuation, Bridge Street, were called the Via Decumana, and Eastgate Street with Watergate Street were called the Via Principalis. They crossed in the centre of the city which was marked in medieval times by the stone 'High Cross'. This stood just in front of St Peter's Church which can be seen towards the left-hand corner of the photograph.

The Industrial Town

The industrial revolution of the nineteenth century caused many towns to grow quickly. They were no longer centres of local trade with some small workshops. Instead they became places which housed a rapidly increasing population who worked in factories.

A nineteenth-century street

Nineteenth-century Features

houses
built in a row
two rooms and kitchen downstairs
two bedrooms upstairs
outside toilet
yard opening on to alleyway at rear
door on to street
sash windows
stone step and window-sills
cellar windows and grating
manhole covers
slate roofs
brick construction
one chimney for open fire in each room

parlour shop
pillar box
cobbles in side street
flagstone pavement
factory with original name
street drains

Modern Features

tarmacadam street surface
road sign
street marking
street lighting
alteration to windows and doors
television aerials
changed use of factory
vehicles
telephone pole and wires

A Nineteenth-century Street

Streets dating from the nineteenth century are typical of our towns and cities because so many were built when the towns grew and expanded. A lot have been pulled down for rebuilding but many, especially from the end of the nineteenth century, still remain. These should be studied for what they can tell us about life at that time.

Study a part of the street. Working in pairs, a group can cover several streets. Make a record of the street as it appears today, either by drawing detailed sketches or by taking photographs. Make a list of all the features dating from the nineteenth century and a separate list of the modern ones. These can be placed on either side of the final copy of your illustration as shown here or can be labelled on to it in two different colours.

Write about the changes that you notice have taken place. Describe or draw what you think the street would have looked like in the nineteenth century.

The Textile Mill

Here is a drawing of William Strutt's cotton mill built in Belper, Derbyshire in 1804.

1   The design of the mill is like a big box with very little decoration. Why is such a design suited to a factory?

2   Why is so much wall space taken up with windows? Why would this be especially important in the nineteenth century?

3   Since it was built this mill has used three different sorts of power. What are they?

4   From the dimensions given, calculate the working area of the factory.

5   One reason for a textile mill having several floors was that it was easier to transmit the power from one source upwards rather than over a long distance horizontally. Give the disadvantages of having a factory on several floors.

6   One disadvantage is the risk of fire. Why should this be so? This particular mill was an early example of a 'fireproof' mill which used iron pillars and beams in its construction.

7   On a copy of the drawing label all the points learned from these questions.

Fieldwork at a textile mill

On a visit to a textile mill see how it compares with William Strutt's mill in design, appearance and size. Draw a diagram and label the important features of the building. If it was originally a water-powered mill, look for and record evidence of this. Where did the mill-workers live? Are the houses of the same date as the mill? Describe the houses in detail.

A Factory Survey

Locate all the factories, workshops and remains of former industry for the whole or part of the town, according to its size. For each place find out the

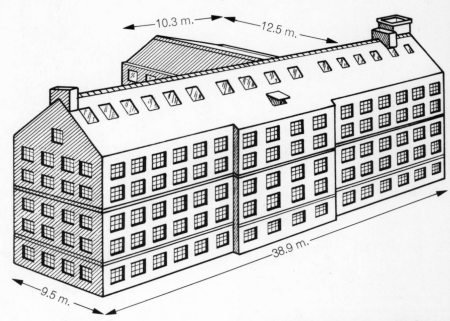

information shown on the sample survey chart. It will be important to draw maps to show: *a.* the location of the factories, the roads, railways and canals
b. the date of the factories
c. the type of industry.

You can now use the information from the maps and questions to tell some of the story of industry in the town.

1   How important is one industry compared with another?

2   How has this importance changed at different times?

Survey chart to be made out for each factory, workshop, or industrial premises

1   Name of factory...

2   Address of factory..

     ....

3   Type of industry...

4   Has the use of this factory or workshop been changed?.............

     ....

5   If so, when was it changed? Date ....

6   What can you find out about the reasons for the change?..........

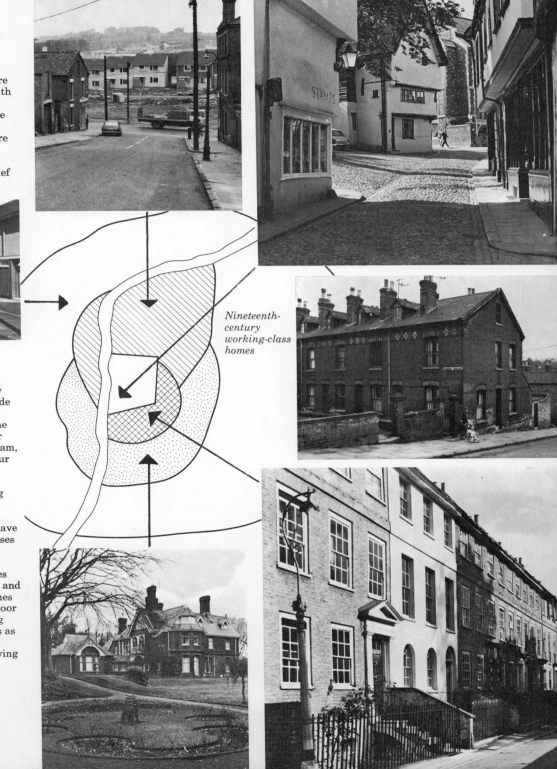

Right: the redevelopment of slums
Far right: a medieval street
Below: a modern housing estate

3 In what ways are the places where factories have been built connected with railways, canals and roads?

4 How has industry spread with the growth of the town?

5 Is one type of industry found more frequently in one location than in another? If so explain why.

6 Find out the reasons why the chief industries of the town grew up here.

Houses

The houses in any town are a lasting record of how it has grown over many centuries. Choose for your study a wide range of houses of different sizes and from different centuries. Obviously the farther you go back in time, the fewer houses there will be. Draw up a diagram, similar to the one given, to record your findings. This will show you how the town has developed.

For each house, study the following aspects: materials, construction, architectural features, date and plan. Look particularly for houses which have changed in their use—very early houses which are perhaps now museums or antique shops; houses which have become offices, schools or flats; houses being cleared for redevelopment. Try and include in your study not only sketches and photographs, but also accurate floor plans and records of lighting, heating and water supply. Notice such things as former accommodation for servants, bathroom conversions, changes in living and garden space.

Right: a Victorian middle-class home
Far right: Georgian houses

Nineteenth-century working-class homes

Shops

Most towns grew up as centres of buying and selling. At first this was done at markets and fairs but gradually the stalls became permanent buildings called shops. Study the shops in your town and see how they have changed through the centuries. Build up a display of information, photographs and drawings from the earliest shops to the present time.

A medieval shop

A medieval shop   Describe the appearance of this shop. Where were the goods made? Where were they sold? Where did the craftsman live? How did he advertise his wares? Where did he display them? What was the difference between a master craftsman, a journeyman and an apprentice? What did the old craft guilds do?

An eighteenth-century shop

An eighteenth-century shop   By this time most craftsmen had moved out of the town centre because of the old guild restrictions. What changes did this bring to the shops? What do we call this type of shop window? Why are these shops so attractive? What sort of goods do such shops usually sell nowadays?

A nineteenth-century parlour shop   Why are these shops so called? Where were they usually sited? What did they sell? What sort of people kept them? Who used them? Why were they so convenient? Why have many had to close down in recent years? When do they do most of their trade?

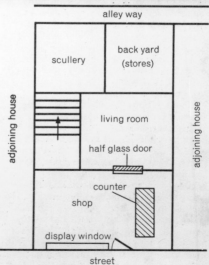

The plan of a nineteenth-century parlour shop